RESEARCH BRIEFINGS 1983

for the Office of Science and Technology Policy,
the National Science Foundation,
and Selected Federal Departments and Agencies

Committee on Science, Engineering,
and Public Policy

National Academy of Sciences

National Academy of Engineering

Institute of Medicine

NATIONAL ACADEMY PRESS
Washington, D.C.   1983

National Academy Press   2101 Constitution Avenue, NW   Washington, DC 20418

This work was supported by the National Science Foundation under Contract PLN-8218330.

Library of Congress Catalog Card Number 83-63234

International Standard Book Number 0-309-03437-X

Committee on Science, Engineering, and Public Policy

Preface

In 1982, on an experimental basis, the National Academies of Sciences and Engineering and the Institute of Medicine, through their joint Committee on Science, Engineering, and Public Policy (COSEPUP), developed research briefings on seven fields of science for the White House Office of Science and Technology Policy (OSTP), the National Science Foundation (NSF), and other interested federal departments and agencies. The seven fields were Mathematics, Atmospheric Sciences, Astronomy and Astrophysics, Agricultural Research, Neuroscience, Human Health Effects of Hazardous Chemical Exposures, and Materials Science. Each briefing, developed by a panel of experts, identified research areas within the field that were likely to return the highest scientific dividends as a result of incremental federal investment in fiscal year 1984. Briefing papers were prepared by each panel and published by the National Academy Press in early 1983.

Shortly thereafter, OSTP and NSF requested a second round of research briefings focused on federal investment opportunities in the fiscal year 1985 budget. COSEPUP agreed to this request and with the assistance of units of the National Research Council and through consultations with OSTP and NSF selected five new research briefing topics. These were as follows:

1. *Selected Opportunities in Chemistry*: Research directed toward enhanced understanding and application of three promising areas of chemistry: understanding chemical reactivity, chemical catalysis, and chemistry of life processes.

2. *Cognitive Science and Artificial Intelligence*: Research directed toward understanding how intelligent systems, animate or inanimate, deal with problems of communication, the acquisition of knowledge, and adaptive behavior.

3. *Immunology*: Research directed toward understanding the molecular, cellular, and intracellular processes of the immune system with a view to understanding control of the immune response and functions of the system.

4. *Solid Earth Sciences*: Research directed toward obtaining a new level of understanding of the structure, composition, energetics, and evolutionary history of the earth, with emphasis on the continental lithosphere and its margins.

5. *Computers in Design and Manufacturing*: Research directed toward understanding and

enhancing the application of computers to product design and manufacture.

This document contains the reports developed on each of these topics.

The second round of briefings was patterned after the first. Each one-hour briefing was developed by a panel of about 12 experts who met once for several days to assess the field and identify areas of unusual scientific opportunity. At each panel meeting a rapporteur was present to summarize the discussions and prepare an initial draft of a briefing paper. After further review by the panels, the briefing papers served as the bases of one-hour oral briefings presented to COSEPUP for review in early August 1983. Based on this review, the briefing papers were revised and served as the bases for oral briefings presented to federal officials in September and October 1983. Separate briefings were provided to Dr. George Keyworth, Science Advisor to the President, and selected members of his staff; Dr. Edward Knapp, Director of the National Science Foundation and senior members of the NSF staff; and senior representatives of other interested federal departments and agencies.

Funds to support both rounds of briefings were provided by the National Science Foundation.

George M. Low, *Chairman*
Committee on Science,
Engineering, and Public Policy

Contents

*Report of the
Research Briefing Panel on
the Solid Earth Sciences*

Research Briefing Panel on the Solid Earth Sciences

Charles L. Drake (*Co-chairman*), Dartmouth College

Don L. Anderson (*Co-chairman*), California Institute of Technology

William R. Dickinson, University of Arizona

Carl Kisslinger, University of Colorado

John C. Maxwell, University of Texas at Austin

V. Rama Murthy, University of Minnesota

Jack E. Oliver, Cornell University

C. Barry Raleigh, Lamont-Doherty Geological Observatory

Frank M. Richter, University of Chicago

Eugene M. Shoemaker, U.S. Geological Survey

Edward M. Stolper, California Institute of Technology

Peter J. Wyllie, California Institute of Technology

Staff

Pembroke J. Hart, *Executive Secretary*, Geophysics Research Forum

Barbara Valentino, *Staff Associate*, Geophysics Research Forum

Patricia Miron, *Secretary*

Allan R. Hoffman, *Executive Director*, Committee on Science, Engineering, and Public Policy

Report of the
Research Briefing Panel on
the Solid Earth Sciences

SUMMARY

The Panel on Solid Earth Sciences has selected five broad targets of opportunity that have the capacity to provide rapid advances in the near future and that will contribute most to our understanding of the Earth's interior and history. The common themes are the structure, composition and evolution of the continental lithosphere, and the dynamics of tectonic processes. This report emphasizes areas that lie on the frontiers of earth sciences—in some cases on the frontiers of chemistry and materials sciences as well—and describes some of the conceptual and technical advances that make it possible to explore more fully the third and fourth dimensions, depth and time. With additional resources, available skills and techniques can be applied immediately to some of these basic problems. Some projects, such as deep continental drilling, determination of the continental geoid, and crustal seismic reflection, can proceed immediately if resources are made available. Others, such as large seismic arrays, expanded isotopic exploration of the crust and mantle, monitoring of crustal motions, and the chemistry and physics of geological materials, require major investments in modern facilities.

With modern facilities and instrumentation the basic research opportunities of these projects will provide excellent training for the next generation of scientific leadership in the earth sciences as well as the advanced skills and trained personnel sought by a wide variety of industries, especially those seeking natural material and energy resources.

INTRODUCTION

Twenty years ago the hypothesis of sea-floor spreading was proposed. It led to general acceptance of the concept of a dynamic Earth and to the plate tectonics model as an explanation for the principal tectonic features. In this model the rigid outer shell of the Earth, the lithosphere, is broken into a limited number of large plates moving relative to one another. Where the plates separate at the ocean ridges new lithosphere is created, which thickens with age and cooling. Where the plates converge—the island arcs and young mountain systems—old ocean lithosphere returns to the deep mantle. Where the plates slide against each other—as in California—

major fault systems develop. Accompanying the interactions of the plate margins are earthquakes, volcanoes, and the concentration of mineral resources.

The importance of this model to the geological sciences can hardly be overstressed. It provided earth scientists for the first time with a working model of the Earth as a whole, a unifying concept of global structure and composition, a fresh context in which to view earth history, and a framework in which to set detailed local investigations.

In succeeding years, development of the model has led to very successful explanations for the development of the oceanic lithosphere and of the major topographic features of the oceans. Through comparative studies of the moon and the terrestrial planets, we have generated a picture of the early history of the Earth and why it appears to be the only one of these bodies on which plate tectonics processes have been active. We are less certain of the nature of the driving forces that move the plates, and we are only beginning to understand the manner in which the continents have been generated and assembled over the last 4 billion years.

In the last decade we have come to recognize that the continents are made up of a large number of microplates assembled over long periods of time. We have found that hydrothermal circulation penetrates deep into the crust and that on ocean ridges the return circulation to the surface may yield metallic sulphide deposits in remarkably short periods of time. We have discovered evidence of major singular events that may have affected the geological record and life on a global scale. We have become able to evaluate the heterogeneity of the mantle, both in physical properties and in chemistry, which has implications with regard to the driving mechanism of plate tectonics and to the formation of continents. In the framework of plate tectonics we have been able to construct generic models to assist us in our search for resources and for a better understanding of the causes of natural hazards.

Technological advances have accompanied these conceptual advances. We can now measure the properties of materials at pressures comparable to those at the center of the Earth. We can perform precise geochemical and isotopic analyses of very small samples of earth materials at levels of 10^{-9} to 10^{-10} grams. Techniques are becoming available that will allow us to monitor crustal motions and positions at the centimeter level of precision. Space techniques have been developed that have permitted us to map the gravity field over the oceans in surprising detail, revealing the fine structure of the sea floor. We can apply tomographic techniques to map the three-dimensional structure of the Earth's interior.

The diversity of approaches within the academic earth sciences is generally well served by the research grant programs of the National Science Foundation (NSF) and, to a lesser extent, of other federal agencies. The Panel strongly supports these programs. In addition, there now exist research opportunities, often large in scale, that are especially timely because technology has become available or because significant progress demands a new approach. Such programs, e.g., scientific drilling or establishment of seismic arrays, are costly and may require considerable investigator collaboration and coordination, but they offer the promise of major increases in our knowledge of the Earth, of how it works and has worked, and of its internal resources.

The scientific problems upon which the recommendations of the Briefing Panel are focused are as follows: (1) *Structure and Composition of the Lithosphere*; (2) *Dynamics of Tectonic Processes*; and (3) *Evolution of the Continental Lithosphere*.

The Panel has based its recommendations on relevant reports by committees of the NAS/NRC, especially the report *Opportunities for Research in the Geological Sciences* prepared at the request of the Director of the Division of Earth Sciences of the National Science Foundation (NSF).

Geoscience research activities of industry

and of federal agencies are often closely intertwined with those of academia, although the goals may differ. Industry has developed technologies and data that are useful in enhancing our basic understanding of the Earth, and it has also applied ideas and techniques developed in academia to its own problems. Many university research activities supported by NSF are dependent on facilities supported or operated by other federal agencies; without these facilities the research cannot be done. At the same time, without support for this research, full advantage cannot be taken of the facilities and graduate students cannot be trained.

The Briefing Panel has identified five research areas in which significant dividends can be expected as a result of incremental federal investment in FY 1985. These five research areas are:

1. Seismic Investigations of the Continental Crust.
2. Continental Scientific Drilling.
3. Physics and Chemistry of Geological Materials.
4. Global Digital Seismic Array.
5. Satellite Geodesy.

ANALYSES OF RECOMMENDATIONS

SEISMIC INVESTIGATIONS OF THE CONTINENTAL CRUST

Seismic investigations include both reflection and refraction seismic surveys, which complement each other. Reflection probing of the continental crust has opened the third dimension to detailed view and has revised our concept of the deep structure of the continental crust and upper mantle. One technique is a modification of petroleum exploration methods. Because of the large service industry involved in the search for petroleum, availability of funds is essentially the only barrier to expansion of this type of exploration. At present only one field crew is being employed full time surveying for sci-

entific purposes in the United States. An augmented effort would provide an opportunity to investigate some of the many attractive target areas that have already been identified as well as to experiment with new ways to apply the technique to obtain greater detail and increased penetration.

Seismic refraction and imaging investigations can use natural (earthquake) or artificial (explosive) sources to probe the continental lithosphere. In this case the research is presently equipment limited. Closely spaced arrays of up to 1000 seismic instruments are required to sample the lithosphere on a scale comparable to its geological heterogeneity. Operation of such an array requires considerable coordination and planning, and these have already begun. Capital investment in portable digital instruments should follow at a rate of 100 instruments per year, and when sufficient instruments have become available a large-scale experiment should begin. Some experiments using new three-dimensional imaging techniques will site the array for several months over particularly interesting areas for determination of deep structure.

The transition from continent to ocean is the fundamental discontinuity in the crust. It takes two major forms: passive margins, which are intraplate, seismically quiet transitions from continental to oceanic crust, and convergent margins, with earthquakes and volcanics, where oceanic lithosphere interacts with that of the continent. The U.S. Geological Survey (USGS), industry, and academic institutions have probed the upper few kilometers of both types of margins, but the deeper structure and the tectonic processes remain a mystery. Innovative applications of existing technology promise to delineate the details of the deeper structure and to allow us to reconstruct the structural, tectonic, and thermal history of these areas.

The most incisive experiments are provided by large seismic (reflection and refraction) arrays. These will require time on ships equipped with seismic reflection instrumen-

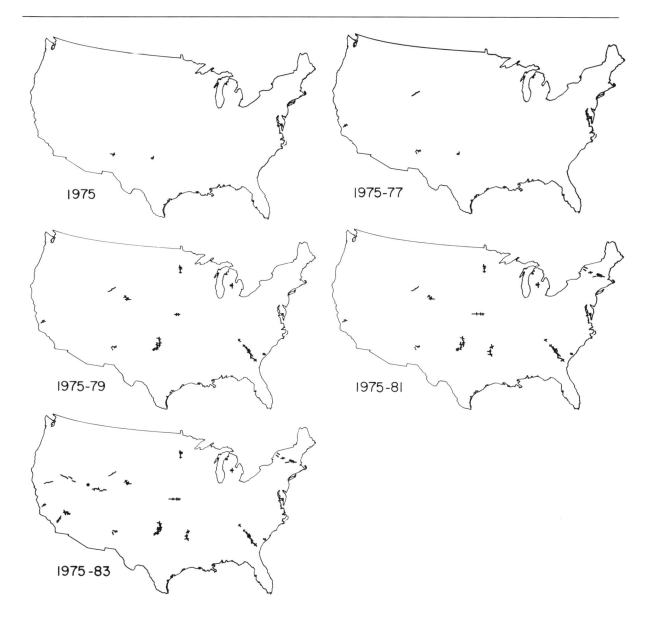

FIGURE 1   COCORP (Consortium for Continental Reflection Profiling) survey lines now total approximately 5200
kilometers.

tation comparable with that available to industry and arrays of ocean bottom seismometers similar to the continental array discussed earlier. On passive margins the continental crust extends as much as 200 kilometers offshore and often contains large sedimentary basins with resource potential. Seismic reflection surveying at sea will provide answers to critically important questions about the origin and evolution of these basins.

CONTINENTAL SCIENTIFIC DRILLING

Drilling in the oceans has revolutionized our ideas about the history and development of these areas; continental scientific drilling promises to be equally exciting.

In the report *Continental Scientific Drilling Program* (NAS/NRC, 1979), four principal problem areas for drilling are identified: thermal regimes; ore-forming processes; understanding earthquakes; and the composition,

6

structure, and time and space relationships of the rocks of the continental crust. Panels of the Continental Scientific Drilling Committee (NAS) have identified priority targets in the these four areas (see Figure 2).

The report *Opportunities for Research in the Geological Sciences* (NAS/NRC) recommends that NSF-funded dedicated continental drilling be initiated in support of numerous research opportunities. This is in addition to scientific drilling carried out by other agencies in support of their missions. Drilling is costly and must be based on well-founded plans for research before, during, and after drilling operations; thus the first requirement is for a national planning and preparation effort for holes dedicated to science. Several regional consortia have already been established, and efforts are under way to establish a national group of which these would be a part.

Many holes are drilled each year for purposes other than scientific research, and some of these are so planned and located that significant information could be gained from add-

on experiments. Several such experiments have been carried out, but the absence of a dedicated budget for such experiments has made it difficult to respond to many of these opportunities in the short time frame that is usually available.

PHYSICS AND CHEMISTRY OF GEOLOGICAL MATERIALS

Measurement of the physical and chemical properties of rocks, minerals, magmas, and aqueous solutions under the extreme conditions of temperature and pressure found in the Earth's interior is required to understand the composition and flow in the mantle, the origin and evolution of magmas, and the evolution and circulation of hydrothermal systems. Similarly, the precise measurement of isotopic ratios of many elements, with techniques developed in the past few years, is needed to trace the secular evolution of igneous rocks and to establish the time constants of various geological processes. An

FIGURE 2 Proposed drill sites, continental scientific drilling committee.

extremely powerful set of techniques for identifying the major chemical reservoirs in the crust and upper mantle tracing materials through transfer processes and for estimating the age of formation of their derived products has been developed. These techniques utilize isotope chemistry and a variety of mass spectrometric instrumentation. A systematic survey of major global rock isotope and geochemistry systems would provide fundamental solutions to many major geological problems.

Progress in these areas depends not only on access to modern technologies and instrument development in the laboratories of chemistry, physics, and material sciences but also on the continuing development of these techniques to make laboratory measurements under the conditions of temperature, pressure, and natural contamination that characterize many geological environments. The high cost of instrumentation in this area and the limited funding available have inhibited the exploitation of rich opportunities.

This country has been a leader in developing the concept of plate tectonics, in applying innovative tools and techniques to studying the Earth and its neighboring planetary bodies, and in developing and manufacturing new instruments. In recent years this leadership posture has been eroded to some degree. A vigorous research program supported by the atomic energy and space efforts equipped many academic laboratories, but no comparable effort in instrumentation has been made for more than a decade. U.S. facilities now show significant obsolescence. If advantage is to be taken of the opportunities that are available in geochemical, isotopic, and high-pressure studies, a major commitment must be made to the development, purchase, and maintenance of new instruments and to the modernization of laboratories.

GLOBAL DIGITAL SEISMIC ARRAY

The seismograph array is the antenna by which the geophysicist receives signals prop-agated by the Earth. The global system of analog instruments has been the main source of data for seismological studies. A small number of digital installations are now in use, supported by DOD, USGS, and NSF; they have confirmed the enormous power of digital data for solving important problems. The goal is to determine the variation of velocity, anelasticity, anisotropy, and stress state through the Earth and, eventually, to map composition and convection.

This goal can be accomplished through a calibrated set of broad-band instruments emplaced around the surface of the globe. An essential element is transmission (near real-time) of the data from about 100 stations by satellite telemetry to a properly equipped data center. All of the technology for achieving this network now exists, but significant support will be required to deploy the system, establish the central receiving and distribution center, upgrade a complementary analog facility, and fund the necessary supporting research.

The Panel recommends that the National Science Foundation act as overall coordinator and lead agency for funding such an array and that the operation be planned and overseen by a university consortium.

SATELLITE GEODESY

The new Global Positioning Satellite (GPS) system promises resolution of position to the centimeter level, giving us the capability of measuring actual plate motion and deformation rather than the results of these integrated over time. Use of GPS will revolutionize both conventional and tectonic, or time-dependent, geodesy.

To take advantage of this new tool, an investment will be required for construction of water-vapor radiometers and to purchase an initial set of GPS receivers for testing the accuracy against existing optical measuring instruments. In subsequent years support will be needed for the acquisition of additional instruments, for field observations, and for the operation of a satellite orbital determination network.

Satellite altimetry (measuring the elevation of the sea surface) recently has been used to construct maps of gravity anomalies in the oceans. These anomalies demonstrate, for example, that fracture zones are much more profound features than had previously been recognized, and they provide direct evidence for shallow convection in the mantle. These measurements will be continued by TOPEX, which is designed principally for oceanographic purposes. The resolution of these measurements can be improved by the systematic measurement of the gravity field from space, as proposed in the Geopotential Research Mission (GRM) of NASA. In addition, a mission such as this can extend high-resolution gravity (and magnetic) measurements to the continents. The value of this mission in providing global gravity coverage and better orbital data for TOPEX and other earlier missions make it an attractive opportunity for an early start.

THE SCIENTIFIC OPPORTUNITIES THAT CAN BE EXPLOITED BY THESE RECOMMENDATIONS

STRUCTURE AND COMPOSITION OF THE CONTINENTAL LITHOSPHERE

In the last few hundred years the two-dimensional surface of the Earth has been explored both geographically and geologically. In this century the third dimension, depth, has been probed intensively in selected areas, particularly the oceans and sedimentary basins, but with limited resolution. Achievements with major impacts on science and society such as development of the concept of plate tectonics and the discovery of major deposits of mineral and energy resources followed this exploration. In this historical context, the next great frontier to be explored clearly seems to be the great body of rocks that form the continental crust and mantle.

Although many modern geological, geophysical, and geochemical studies are compatible with a comparatively simple layered crust, there are increasing indications of complex and discontinuous multilayers, some complexly deformed internally. Exposures of deep crust and samples of deep crust brought up by volcanoes indicate that a variety of sedimentary and volcanic rocks of surficial origin may make up a significant part of the lower as well as the upper crust.

In recent years it has become possible to apply the high-resolution geophysical techniques developed for petroleum exploration to the study of the entire thickness of the continental crust. Although, geographically, only a fraction of the crust has so far been examined, the results reveal a crust of far greater complexity than previously envisioned. In orogenic belts, thin slices of older rock have been thrust for hundreds of kilometers over younger sedimentary rocks of preexisting continental margins. This is an effect of the cycles of opening and closing of ocean basins that seems secondary in terms of basic plate movements but is of primary importance to the development of the continental crust. In areas of active rifting, such as the Basin and Range Province, steeply dipping faults forming and bounding the ranges are found to flatten and to merge at depths with shallow detachment faults that stretch for a hundred or more kilometers beneath the extensional terrain. Such faults may be reactivated zones of weakness from still earlier episodes of major compression and thrust faulting. What is perceived as the fundamental boundary between crust and mantle, the Mohorovicic discontinuity, is clearly far more complex and variable both in vertical and horizontal directions than was commonly thought, and it may vary widely in nature from one locality to another. Faults that may be conduits for mineral-bearing fluids have been traced from surface features, including areas of mineral concentration, to great depths. Molten bodies of rock (magmas) have been mapped at crustal depths where solid rock normally prevails. Deeply buried sediments that are worthy of exploration for petroleum have been found.

The continental crust does not disappear at the shoreline; it extends beneath the continental margins. The margins of the continents vary according to the nature of the processes that have shaped them. Rifting apart of the Atlantic Ocean has left behind a continental shelf in the United States where the evaluation for the potential of oil is dependent on better exploration by refraction and reflection seismic methods. The western margin of Central and North America contains the entire panoply of active plate tectonic processes; rifting in the Gulf of California, subduction of the Pacific plate beneath Central America and the Aleutians, and transcurrent motion from Mexico to northern California. Modern marine seismic methods have advanced rapidly, and these regions are now ripe for intensive exploration.

These new and striking observations of the crust revealed by seismic reflection profiling clearly indicate that a greatly enhanced understanding of the continents will be derived from further observations. Complementary information is derived from wide-angle reflection measurements, refraction measurements on the continents, and the application of newer imaging techniques. To provide measurements with adequate resolution, it is necessary to deploy portable instruments in very large, dense arrays, with up to 1000 instruments, much larger arrays than are currently available or that have been used in past investigations of the lithosphere. These arrays may be employed in refraction profiling using explosive sources, or they can be deployed to monitor earthquake activity over periods ranging from days to months. Such monitoring can provide locations of hypocenters so precise as to permit correlation with specific geological structures at a new level of precision—a level that would significantly advance the understanding of earthquakes and the tectonic processes that cause them. Distant seismic events recorded on these arrays provide the data for deeper imaging.

The ultimate exploration tool, as well recognized by the mineral and petroleum industries, is the drill. Deep-sea drilling has been invaluable in providing verification of geophysical interpretations and has provided detailed information on the structure, composition, and history of the ocean basins. A number of countries have established continental scientific drilling programs, including Canada, France, Belgium, Japan, West Germany, the United Kingdom, Czechoslovakia, and the USSR. The program in the USSR includes a scientific hole in the Kola Peninsula that is now at a depth of 13.5 kilometers (44,000 feet); drilling is continuing with a target of at least 15 kilometers. This is the deepest hole in the world (previous record was 33,000 feet in Oklahoma) and is located entirely in ancient Precambrian rocks. Most of the holes drilled in this country are drilled for water, oil, or minerals. Many are in anomalous areas, where resources are likely to be found; consequently, the basement rocks of the continental crust are unknown in large areas of the country. While some knowledge can be gained by attaching add-on experiments to the holes drilled for other purposes, it is becoming apparent that dedicated holes will be needed to fully understand the structure, composition, and age of the continental crust.

The continental crust and deeper parts of the lithosphere contain the record of about 4 billion years of earth history. The continental crust is also the repository of recoverable resources of minerals and fuels. Many segments of the present continental crust date from a time far back in geological history. There are good physical and chemical reasons to suppose that tectonic regimes and geodynamic mechanisms have changed with time. Important questions arise such as when and how rapidly the continental crust was generated, whether the process was episodic or continuous, and the rate of generation as a function of time.

Studies based on modern isotopic techniques suggest that we are at the threshold of being able to answer some of these questions. It now appears that the continental lithosphere is in some sense complementary to a residual mantle region of global scale. The rate and manner of extraction of continental crustal material from mantle sources can be understood by extensive isotopic and chemical studies of rocks from the upper and lower continental crust. These measurements provide the ages of and information on the nature and history of source materials from which the continental crust has been derived. Present isotopic data suggest that the formation of the continental crust is episodic and that very large volumes are formed in relatively short times.

Finally, in recent years it has been found that the differences between continents and oceans extend to considerable depths (150 kilometers or more) and that the deep structure of the mid-ocean ridges may extend to 400 kilometers. It is not clear whether these differences are statically or dynamically produced, but it is clear that understanding the nature of the continents will require exploration to great depths beneath them. Fortunately, new seismic techniques, similar to medical tomography, can provide this kind of information, both on a regional and a global scale.

Dynamics of Tectonic Processes

Contemporary tectonic theories provide a framework for the synthesis of a wide variety of geological, geophysical, and geochemical data. However, these models are primarily descriptions of operative processes and are only slowly developing into rigorous and quantitative formulations. Increased amounts of new and high-quality data; advances in continuum mechanics, materials science, and other relevant physics; and availability of adequate computers make the present time right for rapid progress toward the development of more effective models of structural processes.

Research in tectonics is carried out in the field, where nature is observed; in the laboratory, where the myriad parameters in the real world can be controlled; and through theoretical studies. Laboratory studies of rock deformation tell us about processes in rocks and the changes that result from high deviatoric stress. The changes caused by stress provide a basis for interpreting geodetic and geophysical data in tectonically active areas. Seismic techniques are being applied to the determination of magnitude and orientation of stress in the mantle. Studies of petrofabrics in the field and in the laboratory provide clues to the temperature, stress, and flow conditions that prevailed during the formation of the rock. Thus we can study past as well as contemporary dynamics of the lithosphere and the underlying mantle.

The data critical to establishing the kinematics of plate motion were based on paleomagnetic studies and marine geophysical measurements. Now, with the remarkable accuracy of new Global Positioning Satellite receivers, we can foresee that within a few years plate velocity vectors can be determined and accelerations in plate motion can be measured. The interaction of the plates in great earthquakes can be observed directly by measurement of earthquake displacements and post-seismic dissipation of strain. This new, relatively inexpensive technology provides one of the most exciting opportunities in the earth sciences today.

Knowledge of the stresses in the lithosphere is fundamental to understanding the physics of tectonic processes. Because it is a tensor quantity describing forces internal to a mass of material, stress is difficult to observe directly. Overcoring and hydrofracturing techniques have been used for in situ measurements of stress in rocks, but only the latter is useful at significant depths. The cost of hydrofracturing rises steeply with depth because of the need to drill a hole; therefore, stress measurements should be included in the observation program for all deep holes drilled for scientific purposes. New holographic techniques are being developed for down-hole applications.

Stress measurements at isolated points are the beginning step in analysis, but it is the spatial variation in stress that drives dynamic processes. Because earthquakes are the result of stresses at the source, both the radiated waves and the permanent deformation they produce contain important information on stress. Seismic source theory and wave propagation theory are sufficiently developed that the dynamic and geometric properties of the sources can be derived routinely from analysis of sets of seismograms. This is done in the time domain by matching the calculated and observed waves and in the frequency domain by interpreting the spectral characteristics. The greatest need is for high-quality digital data from earthquakes with a wide spread of geographical distribution and magnitudes. The technology exists; it is a matter of deploying the instruments and creating the data management facilities to serve the experimenters.

Digital data are also required for the analysis of elastic wave velocity anisotropy. Interpretation of anisotropy data is more ambiguous than waveform analysis because it can result from both deviatoric stresses and crystal alignment. Crystal alignment in rocks of the mantle is itself the result of flow; thus, it can shed light on internal dynamic processes. These anisotropy studies have the advantage that they can be used to probe any region through which the waves travel, not just tectonically active areas. Detection of anisotropy from wave polarization anomalies and surface wave dispersion is being recognized as a powerful tool for studying Earth dynamics; the availability of large quantities of broadband digital data will enhance development of this approach. Similarly, the attenuation of seismic waves is controlled by temperature and dislocation structure and, thus, stress.

Finally, the response of rocks to stresses is governed by their rheological properties. More complete knowledge of the elastic and inelastic mechanical and thermodynamic proper-

ties of the materials in the crust and mantle is needed as a basis for modeling processes ranging from metamorphism to basin formation and mountain building. New laboratories need to be built to measure the elastic and anelastic properties of minerals at extreme conditions and to synthesize materials at high pressure and temperature. These are frontier areas of materials science.

Dynamics and Structure of the Earth's Interior

The Earth's mantle and core are the major components of its interior. From geophysical studies, experimental investigations reaching the temperature and pressure conditions of the core-mantle boundary, geochemical and isotopic analysis of mantle-derived rocks, and modeling, we have obtained a rough understanding of the composition and physical state of the mantle and the core.

Plate tectonics and related phenomena result from flow in the mantle. This flow is also the principal process by which heat escapes from the Earth's interior. Beneath a rigid outer shell—the lithosphere—the Earth's mantle, which responds like a solid to short-term driving forces, behaves as a fluid over geological time. Plate motions are the result of convection in the mantle, but the pattern of convection is controversial; some advocate whole-mantle convection, others suggest separate systems in the upper and lower mantle. It is not known whether mantle convection occurs on a scale that is small compared to the large-scale flow associated with plate motions and whether the time dependence associated with the plate configurations is the only time-dependent aspect of plate tectonics.

It has been difficult to place observational constraints on the flow in the Earth's interior. However, techniques are now available for mapping of the Earth's interior in three dimensions (elastic wave tomography). One approach involves the systematic inversion of large amounts of travel-time data of compressional and shear waves that have traveled through the Earth; the other involves modeling based on free oscillations and surface waves having periods sufficiently long to be affected by the deep interior. Both approaches require large computing facilities and a global array of broad-band digital seismometers. Higher-resolution studies require large transportable arrays.

Recent advances in theory and increases in computational capacity are available to help solve the fundamental flow problems. Most models of mantle flow have been based on a single layer behaving as a Newtonian fluid. Mantle silicates have strong temperature- and stress-dependent rheologies and the mantle is surely inhomogeneous in viscosity and probably in chemistry. Melting that occurs in the course of convection affects the buoyancy. It is now possible to compute flow in a layered system with these complications taken into account; preliminary results are providing insight into the dynamics of the interior. When continents are present on the surface it may be that steady-state never prevails. The required three-dimensional finite element calculations exceed the capacity of most university computers and computer budgets, but they must be made if the understanding of mantle dynamics is to proceed beyond the present qualitative stage.

In addition to seismological data, data on the global geoid, gravity and topography, crustal and sedimentary rock thickness, and heat flow are also pertinent to investigations of mantle flow, rheology, and evolution. Of special value among newly available data are satellite-borne radar measurements of the shape of the sea surface (geoid). There are satellite techniques for extending this high-resolution geoid to the continents. Systematic treatment of these data will make it possible to place bounds on the locations of density and velocity anomalies in the mantle. Explanation of the geoid is one of the most challenging problems of modern earth science. If we understood the geoid, we should know whether the rheology of the mantle is strongly temperature and stress dependent,

whether the convection is layered or whole mantle, and whether convection is statistically steady. It has been suggested recently that the geoid has a memory—that its present shape reflects conditions in the distant past. If this is true, then we have the exciting prospect of being able to identify past configurations of the continents, ridges, and subduction zones.

Laboratory measurements of the rheology of melts and silicate minerals at high temperatures and controlled dislocation densities are an essential part of these studies. Experimental geophysics has gone through a decline in recent years, in part because of obsolescence of equipment. New laboratories, filling the gap between rock mechanics and ultrasonics, are required to provide the basis for interpreting seismic attenuation and anisotropy observations in terms of rheology, stress, and flow.

A major advance in our understanding of the mantle has been the discovery that the mantle is chemically heterogeneous on a variety of scales. Evidence of this is provided by the precise analysis of Pb, Sr, Nd, and He isotopes of young volcanic rocks from the oceans. These data show that the mantle sources that yield mid-ocean ridge basalts (MORB) have been isolated and depleted, relative to other sources of basaltic rocks, in their radioactive and other trace elements for a period on the order of 1.5 to 2.0 billion years. Furthermore, the mantle sources that produce MORB appear to be a distinct global entity: relatively homogeneous chemically but distinct from all other mantle sources that produce basalts. For example, basalts from major volcanic centers on oceanic islands and from continental interiors cover a broad geochemical and isotopic range. The sources of these so-called hotspot magmas are enigmatic. Investigations in this area have been limited. Few laboratories are working on these fundamental problems because of the expense of establishing and maintaining modern isotopic facilities and their supporting high-precision separation and analytic equipment.

Modern labs have recently been set up in England, France, West Germany, Australia, and Japan, often by U.S.-trained investigators.

Magma Genesis and Fluid Flow

Igneous activity—melting in the Earth's interior, migration of magmas toward the Earth's surface, eruption on the surface or emplacement at depth—is the major process of crustal formation and one of the major mechanisms of heat and mass transfer in the outer regions of the Earth. It is the principal mechanism by which volatiles are transported to the surface to form the atmosphere and hydrosphere; cooling of magma bodies sets up hydrothermal systems that produce some of our most vital mineral deposits. Volcanic eruption of magmas may present a significant hazard, but the study of the solidified products of magmas provides clues about conditions in the Earth's interior and their evolution. Generation of magmas not only results from convective upwelling but also, through phase transformations, may influence the density structure of the mantle and provide a positive feedback on the convective process itself.

Investigation of magmas requires a strong combination of field and laboratory studies, but the most significant recent advances have come from development and application of tools from physics, chemistry, and material science to the problems. We can now, in the diamond cell, measure the properties of minerals and fluids under static pressures up to 1.5 megabars and from cryogenic temperatures to 3000° C; we can study the speciation and kinetics of aqueous solutions similar in composition to ore-forming hydrothermal solutions; we can study crystalline and amorphous materials from new perspectives using newly developed or accessible spectroscopic techniques and surface techniques from the materials sciences. These developments suggest that future advances will be led by the new types of and higher-quality data made available through application of innovative analytical and experimental techniques.

Theoretical studies of fluid flow have also played an important role in modifying current thinking about processes in the lithosphere. Fluid dynamic modeling of magma migration in the mantle and crust and of circulation of aqueous fluids in the crust, including the progressive chemical interactions taking place during fluid flow and their feedback on the flow processes, are in their infancy. Preliminary results suggest potential breakthroughs in understanding the factors responsible for mineral-deposit formation and many of the observed chemical and eruptive characteristics of magmas. Such models are critically constrained by geochemical and isotopic measurements on "fossilized" circulation systems and magmas and by measurements of permeability of rocks and the physical and chemical properties of rocks, magmas, and hydrothermal fluids. The systematic application of isotopic techniques to the study of natural stable and unstable isotopic systems is critical. Field investigations, including deep sampling by drilling, and laboratory studies of rocks and model systems are needed to provide realistic constraints and inputs into such studies.

High-Pressure Geophysics

Our understanding of the constitution of the Earth's upper mantle is based primarily on interpretations of seismic data and on the study of igneous and metamorphic rocks believed to have been brought up from relatively great depths by volcanic activities. At deeper levels (greater than 200 kilometers), where our only probes are seismic waves and interpretations of the geoid, realistic interpretations in terms of actual mineralogy, composition, temperature, and rheology require measurements of the physical properties of individual minerals and aggregates at temperatures and pressures relevant to the mantle. Elastic constants and their pressure and temperature derivatives, rheological properties, and phase relations are vital to these considerations. Facilities for synthesis of large volumes of high-pressure phases in order to determine thermodynamic and elastic properties are available (principally outside the United States), and new opportunities are now available for studying the physical and chemical properties in the diamond cell under extreme conditions of temperature and pressure. Such measurements include scattering and reemission (e.g., Raman, fluorescence), diffraction (e.g., X-ray, Brillouin), and absorption spectroscopy (e.g., Mossbauer effect, visible, and infrared). Such measurements are essential not only for interpretation of seismic and gravity data but also as input into realistic models of convection in the Earth's interior.

EVOLUTION OF THE CONTINENTAL LITHOSPHERE

Our concepts of the manner of evolution of the Earth and its life have been heavily based on the gradualist ideas of Lyell and Darwin. Recently this manner of biological evolution has been questioned, and it has been suggested that it is not gradual, but punctuated; singular events may play a major role in determining the evolution of organisms. When we consider the evolution of continents we find a similar situation. One can explain the shaping of the Earth's surface as the result of slow processes; mountains appear to be built in geologically short intervals of time separated by long periods of relative quiescence. The average integrated rate of plate movements, measured paleomagnetically, is a few centimeters per year, but current activity along the plate margins is episodic, with earthquakes followed by quiescence; periods of intense volcanism followed by periods of little activity. Singular events, such as the great explosions of Yellowstone, Long Valley, or the Valles calderas, located within the continental mass, are anomalous in terms of a simple gradualistic model.

The continents, with their great age and complexity, carry within them not only most of the Earth's exploitable energy and mineral resources but also clues to the Earth's long history. In contrast, although the rocks of the ocean's floor are relatively young (less than 200 million years), they provide us with the keys to plate tectonics. The great ocean rifts are the primary distillery for separation of the lighter fractions of the mantle into the ocean crust.

The ancient cores of the continents are fringed by younger belts that have been added in the last billion years. In some zones of collision, accretion to the continent of shingles of overthrusted oceanic crust and sediment has contributed to continental growth, while the denser mantle has descended below the continental lithosphere. Study of the accretionary process at the margins of the continents needs to be augmented by extensive examination through geological and geophysical methods and, ultimately, by drilling.

The steady accretion process is punctuated by collisions of continents and by episodes of rifting of the continental lithosphere to create new continental margins and new ocean basins. Sedimentary basins, often containing hydrocarbons, form over these rifts, and the sediments contain the evidence of the rifting process and subsequent subsidence. Rifting has been pervasive during the last billion years, but many of the rifts cease their activity and do not become continental margins. The eastern continental margin is an outstanding example of a successful rift. Its shallower portions have been studied extensively for scientific and petroleum exploration purposes, but understanding of its deeper regions and its full history await clarification by advanced seismic techniques and drilling.

The continental blocks now appear to have been assembled through the course of time from small fragments, some broken off other continents. Examples of this phenomenon have been best identified both on the eastern and the western parts of the country but are evident elsewhere. A broad spectrum of techniques can be brought to bear on identification of these fragments: paleomagnetism;

15

geochemistry and isotope geology; field mapping; structural and stratigraphic studies; and, where the rocks are buried, seismic measurements and drilling.

Prior to one billion years ago, the evidence for modern plate tectonics processes becomes more obscure. This is not surprising, as the record itself becomes more limited. Processes other than those associated with plate tectonics as we understand them may have contributed to the formation of continental blocks. At the present, two opposing hypotheses can be entertained: that the processes of plate tectonics, operating over a long period of time, have caused the gradual emergence of continental crust from the mantle, and that most of the volume of continental crust was generated early in the Earth's history by processes lacking modern analogs.

To answer this fundamental question we will have to draw on all of our tools—geological, geophysical, and geochemical. Within the major parts of the crust, continent and ocean, and the mantle and core, large-scale geochemical heterogeneities or reservoirs have appeared since the formation of the Earth. The number, size, spatial arrangement, and evolution of reservoirs capable of yielding distinctly different magmas constitute a matter of vigorous debate. In addition, the nature and magnitude of fluxes between reservoirs are poorly known but are essential to understanding the chemical and differentiation history of the Earth. For example, some oceanic basalts have been interpreted as retaining geochemical signatures of recycled ancient ocean crust, raising the question of whether differentiation of the mantle is proceeding irreversibly or whether it is approaching a steady state with recycling.

Characterization of the reservoirs can be greatly advanced by the simultaneous measurement of the Nd/Sm and Rb/Sr isotopic systems together with measurements on the same sample of uranium, thorium, lead, and oxygen isotopes and trace-element abundances. A variety of other isotope systems is now being exploited. The measurement of rare gases, particularly $^3He/^4He$, has shown that mantle reservoirs may not be totally outgassed; components that have not previously been on the Earth's surface are still being supplied from the interior. The distribution and evolution of geochemical reservoirs are intimately related to the dynamics of the plate-mantle system and to the thermal and tectonic evolution of the Earth and its continents. The trace-element and isotopic chemistry of crustal and mantle magmas and rocks are essential petrological data, yet only a few laboratories in this country are equipped to make these measurements.

CONCLUSION

Early investigation of the Earth required keen observational powers and a knowledge of the composition of rocks and minerals, of the distribution of organisms through time, and of fundamental geological processes. Through these investigations we gained understanding of the near-surface geology and we were able to exploit this knowledge to obtain resources from the Earth. Similarly, we were able to determine the gross features of the Earth's interior, first through geophysical observations and, more recently, through geochemical and geophysical experimentation and isotopic studies.

The solid Earth interacts with all of the other domains of the geosphere: oceans, atmosphere, solar terrestrial. It is the sole source of information regarding the history of actions and reactions of the geosphere and biosphere. Improved knowledge of the solid Earth and the processes that operate within it are significant not only to basic science but also to society. We live on the solid Earth; we extract our resources from it; it produces the magnetic field through internal motions; from it came the gases of the atmosphere, the waters of the sea and the salts contained within them, and the nutrients that feed its organisms. Terra firma usually describes it well, but internal and external forces produce changes with significant impact on society.

Our tools have become sharper in recent years, and advances in theory and technology provide us with new opportunities to explore in greater detail the nature of and processes in the interior of the Earth as well as the development of the Earth through time. The availability of modern instrumentation and techniques will contribute to the training of the next generation of scientific leadership in the solid earth sciences and of the personnel sought by government and industry to assess hazards and resources.

Report of the
Research Briefing Panel on
Cognitive Science and Artificial Intelligence

Research Briefing Panel on
Cognitive Science and Artificial Intelligence

William K. Estes (*Co-chair*), Harvard
University
Allen Newell (*Co-chair*), Carnegie-Mellon
University
John R. Anderson, Carnegie-Mellon
University
John Seely Brown, Xerox Palo Alto Research
Center
Edward A. Feigenbaum, Stanford
University
James Greeno, University of Pittsburgh
Patrick J. Hayes, University of Rochester
Earl Hunt, University of Washington, Seattle
Stephen M. Kosslyn, Harvard University
Mitchell Marcus, Bell Telephone
Laboratories

Shimon Ullman, Massachusetts Institute of
Technology

Staff

Paul S. Rosenbloom, *Rapporteur*, Carnegie-
Mellon University
David A. Goslin, *Executive Director*,
Commission on Behavioral and Social
Sciences and Education
Sarah M. Streuli, *Administrative Secretary*,
Commission on Behavioral and Social
Sciences and Education
Allan R. Hoffman, *Executive Director*,
Committee on Science, Engineering, and
Public Policy

20

Report of the
Research Briefing Panel on
Cognitive Science and Artificial Intelligence

Start with a fundamental question that arose with the scientific world view: How can mind exist in a world totally governed by physical law? Shift that question, with the coming of experimental psychology: What laws and regularities govern human behavior? Convert that question, with the growing understanding of biology: How can the brain give rise to all the phenomena that we call mental? Expand that question, with the emergence of computer science: What is the general nature of intelligent action, independent of the device (brain, computer, etc.) by which it is implemented? All these questions reflect a single underlying great scientific mystery, on a par with understanding the evolution of the universe, the origin of life, or the nature of elementary particles.

Nothing short of a full history of Western intellectual endeavor can make sense of the crazy quilt of disciplines devoted to facets of this fundamental question, each in its own way. Cognitive science and artificial intelligence stand together in taking information processing as the central activity involved in intelligent behavior and in taking the framework of modern computer science as the foundation for understanding information-processing systems. Cognitive science reflects a concern with how humans process information, being an offshoot of cognitive psychology, linguistics, and philosophy. Artificial intelligence reflects a concern with how computers process information, being a part of computer science. The rapid growth of these disciplines in recent years is advancing our understanding of the nature of mind and the nature of intelligence on a scale that is proving revolutionary.

The research cited in this report reflects three main themes:

1. Answering the fundamental scientific question of the nature of intelligence and how it arises out of primitive cognitive functions. A subtheme, but one pregnant with hope, is the joining of this understanding with work in neuroscience, to make new progress in grounding the mechanisms of intelligence in the mechanisms of the brain.
2. Solving increasingly complex problems by constructing computer systems with the requisite intellectual, perceptual, and learning powers—making full use of the increasing speeds and memory being provided by hardware technology.
3. Developing human talent by combining

an understanding of how humans learn and perform cognitive tasks with effective intelligent systems to aid this development.

THE DOMAIN OF COGNITIVE SCIENCE AND ARTIFICIAL INTELLIGENCE

How can we characterize this broad field? Look first at what investigators are typically found to be doing. An investigator in artificial intelligence is constructing a computer program that can detect trends and constancies in data and induce physical laws. The program (aptly called *Bacon*) has rediscovered Kepler's third law of planetary motion and Galileo's law for the pendulum, among others. The investigator is trying to produce a program that can accomplish a task requiring kinds of reasoning hitherto presumed to be the province solely of human intelligence. He is also progressing toward discovery programs of greater generality through the evaluation and improvement of the approximate rules (heuristics) used to guide the program in its search for physical laws.

A cognitive psychologist is measuring the speed with which people can carry out mental operations on visual images—for example, rotating a figure in imagination—and observes that the time required to rotate a figure mentally is proportional to the angle of rotation, as specified externally. The investigator is testing hypotheses about the form in which information is represented in images and working toward a model capable of simulating the way mental operations on images enter into reasoning and problem solving.

The scope of the combined field of cognitive science and artificial intelligence is much wider than suggested by these two illustrations. In one direction are formal investigations of the abstract properties of computational systems that are basic to all intelligent behavior. In another are experimental studies of human observers detecting signals of millisecond duration in noisy backgrounds. In yet another direction are analyses of verbal communications to find the rules whereby people resolve ambiguities in language.

The common core of these diverse enterprises may be taken to be the task of understanding intelligence and intelligent behavior. What might we expect of a general theory of intelligence? Most immediately, it should help us to understand how the constituents of intelligent function have evolved in the human mind, the limits they set on possible achievement, the potentialities that are open to improvement. At the same time, the theory should help us understand how computers can carry out human-like activities and the ways in which they may exceed human capabilities. More broadly, an adequate theory of intelligence should guide attacks on questions or issues that go beyond our ordinary experience. Considering the current searches by some physicists and astronomers for evidence of intelligent life elsewhere in the universe, would we recognize intelligence in organisms very different from ourselves? Is it possible to set any theoretical limits on the possible differences in level or quality of intelligent function? Is human intelligence subject to biological constraints that do not apply to artificial systems?

ORIGINS

Artificial intelligence has been a recognized field of study for only a little over 25 years. Its theoretical substrate was the development of ideas regarding mathematical logic and computation during the 1930s and 1940s. The rapid development of digital computers from 1950 on provided a challenge to get these machines to accomplish tasks that had previously been the sole province of human intelligence. The computer provided, for the first time, a mechanism whereby theories of intelligent performance could be rigorously defined, built, and tested—providing the feedback necessary for rapid progress. The first efforts were the well-known attempts to program computers to play intellectual games, notably chess. But as it became clear that intelligence was based on the ability to process symbols and that computers were general symbol manipulators rather than just high-speed numerical calculators, the scope of efforts rapidly broadened to include research into induction, problem solving, theorem proving in logic, language understanding, and vision.

Cognitive science emerged into public view in the late 1970s, as an interdisciplinary field to cover all the sciences adopting an information-processing approach.* It did not come out of thin air. Seventy-five years of work by experimental psychologists brought human cognition into the laboratory and developed models sufficient to enable meaningful measures of the speed of mental operations and the amounts of information stored in memory following a learning experience. However, the ability to address how people deal with problems much more complex than those of simple laboratory tasks came with two developments of the 1960s.

The first was a suitable conceptual framework for a science of cognition. Developments in computer science and artificial intelligence gave rise to the view of the human as an information processor—a special kind of processor perhaps, but still one sharing basic principles and constraints with computer-based information-processing systems. The computer made clear how to partition the staggering task of comprehending the human mind and brain in all their aspects into two more tractable components. The critical idea was the distinction between computer hardware and software. One can learn how a computer works by studying its hardware—its electrical circuitry, recording medium, and timing mechanisms. With little knowledge of such matters, one can master the software and become a highly skilled programmer.

In the study of human intelligence, the scientific objective is to construct a theoretical picture of the structures and processes of human cognitive function at the level corresponding to software—the theoretical notions referring to the way information becomes encoded and organized in memory, the cognitive operations available for accessing and transforming the information, and the functional principles governing the sequencing and combination of operations. Cognitive scientists continue to hope for the ultimate explanation of mental phenomena at lower levels of scientific analysis, but they have found out how to proceed toward the development of useful theories without waiting on developments in neuroscience. These cognitive theories are thoroughly mechanistic, even though the mechanisms are not yet related to how they are realized in the brain.

The second main source of concepts and methods for the new cognitive science came from advances in linguistics. The importance of language in human thought has always been recognized in a general way. But the beginnings of a clear understanding of what it means to know a language, and therefore the first possibility of discovering how languages are learned and used, flowed from developments in theoretical linguistics in the 1960s, in particular Chomsky's formulation of generative grammars—sets of abstract rules that produce exactly the set of grammatical sentences. Increasingly sophisticated and psychologically relevant theories of grammar have provided a framework for interpreting studies of language-based cognitive activity and posed in clear and researchable form the major problem of how the understanding of language is achieved and how language is acquired by the young.

FROM THEORY TO RESEARCH

Research in artificial intelligence and cognitive science is strongly theory driven.

---

*As such, artificial intelligence is included in cognitive science; we have kept them separate here to emphasize the joining of human and engineering disciplines.

Increasingly, empirically oriented research is aimed at finding evidence relative to general theories rather than being a process of accumulating empirical facts and attempting to induce laws or principles. Thus a look at theoretical issues concerning system design and function will lead directly to the principal lines of research within which we can identify special opportunities with a high yield from increased efforts.

System Design

In artificial intelligence, system design refers to the relation between the way computers are constructed and the kinds of programs that can be implemented on them. The key concept is the *architecture*, which is the structure of the machine that permits it to be programmed—thus, the structure that creates the distinction just discussed between hardware and software. Any particular part of a system can be implemented in either hardware or software, with the choice to be made on the basis of trade-offs involving implementation cost, speed of execution, frequency of use, functionality, and flexibility. A critical question is what mechanism must be included in the hardware in order for the system to be able to manifest intelligent capabilities. What mechanisms, if not built into the architecture, would make basic intelligent capabilities (such as learning and problem solving) too difficult or slow to be feasible?

We have come to understand that one major aspect of the architecture is that it provides for *symbolic* behavior. That is, it permits computers to have internal representations that *refer* to other things. The computer's symbols (which are basically its addresses and operation codes) seem special, referring only to data structures in its own memories and to its own information processes. Yet out of that mode of reference comes the ability to refer to things in the outside world—to objects, activities, events, and abstract concepts. The internal symbols access data structures plus programs that interpret the data structures as representing the external thing. These data structures and programs were constructed by processes that had information about the outside thing. Because of this we ourselves can program computers to deal with many things—anything to which we set our mind. But systems themselves can also construct such symbols and their meanings when given information about the external object. Thus, for the first time we see how symbols and symbolic behavior can be realized in a physical system.

The hypothesis that links artificial intelligence and human cognition together, providing the frame within which scientific inquiry proceeds, holds that all intelligence, including human intelligence, arises from the ability to use symbols. By symbols we mean the physical symbol systems, noted above, as first understood in computer science. Without this stipulation the hypothesis would constitute only another version of the long-held view that symbols are important in human mental life. But with the notions of symbol and symbol system firmly connected to the physical world via the realization in computers, the hypothesis anchors the study of all the higher processes of mind to the same scientific world of mechanism as all other natural sciences.

Much is known about the abstract structure of such symbol systems (so-called universal computational systems), so the linking hypothesis is not that somehow the human is like a computer but that both humans and computers embody these systems and gain, thereby, their ability for intelligence and information processing.

Whereas the architecture of a computer is determined by the designer, the architecture of the human cognitive system is given by nature, and discovering its properties presents a major scientific challenge. For instance, it is evident that a human does not carry out actions the way current computers do, by a simple interpretive cycle of fetching the next instruction and then executing it. Rather, the human is much more recognition driven, with the current situation (at each instant), including the goals and momentarily active memory, directly determining the next action to be taken. The human cognitive system seems to be highly general-purpose, taking on a particular shape only in the course of adapting to the demands of a specific task. But structural constraints—those aspects of the cognitive architecture that determine which intelligent functions are easy or difficult to perform—are clearly of major importance. We know the human brain has many highly developed special structures for specific functions. Resolving the nature of these constraints is a prime task for research in cognitive science.

SYSTEM FUNCTION

In artificial intelligence the computer is made to take on intelligent function by programming it within the framework provided by the architecture. The endless diversity of intelligent behavior stems from the ability of an intelligent system to program itself—to create symbolic structures to guide its own future behavior. Programmability per se does not make evident how the intelligence is attained, even given a suitable architecture. What sort of programming leads to intelligent action? This too is now clear in outline. The two basic ingredients are search and knowledge.

Search arises by defining a space of possibilities large enough to contain the sought-for solution and then searching for the solution by generating the states of the space. Thus arises the familiar exponentially expanding search of potential future chess positions by chess programs as well as the search of possible isomers of a given chemical formula by the *Dendral* program in searching for an isomer that satisfies the mass spectrogram data of an unknown sample, thus discovering its structural formula. Indeed, all the basic methods of intelligence appear to involve search.

Knowledge is necessary to guide the search

through the space—to avoid having to find the proverbial needle in a haystack. A prominent component of artificial intelligence systems is the memory organizations that hold the knowledge and permit finding the right bit of knowledge at the right time. For instance, much of the progress in the development of expert systems—programs capable of exhibiting expert-level performance in intellectual domains—has come from discovering that large amounts of how-to knowledge can be effectively represented by collections of *if-then* rules (productions), where each rule of behavior carries the conditions in which it is to apply (the if-part) as well as what it is supposed to do (the then-part). In contrast to how-to knowledge, bodies of factual knowledge are organized into networks of associations, so that access to part of the knowledge base provides the connections to obtain other relevant parts. These networks go beyond the simple concept of association. For example, they must be organized such that widely applicable knowledge is not redundantly stored with each specific object to which it applies. Knowledge about an automobile must be composed of what is specific to the car (its dents) plus knowledge about all cars of that make. But the latter is similarly composed of knowledge specific to the make-plus knowledge about cars in general. This progression continues up through the most general nature of physical objects, imposing a hierarchical as well as an associational structure on the knowledge. The discovery of these forms of representation and memory organization and their efficacy for wide classes of tasks constitutes important scientific knowledge about intelligent systems.

Beyond matters of organization is the question of content. For a computer system to solve problems about cars, it must know about cars—and not just the specific facts about Fords and Chevies but all the concepts that make up the domain, such as steering, carburetors, that motors heat up, what a motor is, what heat is, and so on. Artificial intelligence systems differ from more standard computer applications precisely in that the knowledge involved in the system is not highly circumscribed. By the same coin, our current artificial intelligence systems, despite much progress, are still woefully limited in their knowledge compared to what general intelligence requires. Obtaining the knowledge to incorporate in systems is itself a major scientific task. This is especially true of expertise. One of the interesting results to come out of the work on expert systems is that experts cannot explain in general to another person the knowledge behind their ability to make expert choices. Only when put into concrete choice situations can they evoke reasons for their particular choice, and these reasons must then be integrated into a total organization (as in the *if-then* rules above).

Intelligence is shaped to an important extent by the properties of the languages and representations that it employs. Human intelligence is intimately involved with natural language (e.g., English), and in this respect it contrasts with the programming-language representations available in computers. The extent of the resulting constraints on human thinking and the degree to which they can be incorporated in computers are not yet fully understood. Human thought is also involved to an important, and perhaps not fully appreciated, extent with imagery. A new line of research in cognitive science is the investigation of models that may enable us to understand the "language" of the imagery system.

MAJOR RESEARCH AREAS

With the background above, we can now turn to specific areas of research.

Architectures

It should be apparent from the discussion so far that architecture is a key concept for cognitive science and artificial intelligence, bringing in its train a large number of signif-icant notions. Research into architectures is an active and important part of the field.

Computer Architectures

The most active research on architectures is in artificial intelligence rather than cognitive science. This effort is concerned with discovering the best architectures to support powerful problem-solving and learning mechanisms. Not only must computers be created with immense power (artificial intelligence supercomputers), but many organizational issues in the architecture are still to be discovered and understood. For example, how should memory be structured and accessed so that contact can be made between a novel situation and stored knowledge and problem-solving methods? How can new information be integrated into existing memory structures so that the system can learn through experience? Research into such topics translates directly into more powerful applied systems. It also provides a fund of knowledge about possible mechanisms upon which theories of human cognition can be built.

Massive Parallelism

The study of massively parallel systems has recently emerged as a major focus of architectural research. Originally, of course, computers were primarily uniprocessors (and artificial intelligence research concentrated on aspects, such as problem solving, that were primarily serial). But for some time computer science has been devoting major attention to how to exploit parallel computation, driven by the increasing difficulty in developing ever faster circuits and attracted by the emergence of integrated-circuit technologies that favor parallelism. There are many flavors of parallelism, varying with the number of concurrent processors, the intimacy of communicative coupling between the processors (measured by the instructions performed between significant interactions), and the volume of data flowing between them.

Massively parallel architectures are designed to have many simple processors (millions), with each one dedicated to a conceptual entity represented in the system. This contrasts with current architectures (including parallel ones) that dedicate a segment of memory to each conceptual entity but share processing capacity by shipping each piece of data to a processor for its moment of modification. The immediate research problem is learning how to compute effectively with these million-fold parallel architectures. However, the research vista that structures of this new class open up for cognitive science and artificial intelligence is more than just the hope of increased power. This class of architectures makes new contact with biological computation, which is also massively parallel. Indeed, the work is being deliberately guided by biological systems, especially the visual system.

Human Cognitive Architecture

Whereas in computer science and artificial intelligence, research on architectures takes the form of designing architectures and investigating their properties, in cognitive science the approach must be to hypothesize possible architectures and discover whether their implications for cognitive processes accord with empirical observation. The task is formidable because the university of plausible hypotheses is immense, and properties of architectures are only remotely connected to observable behavior. A major step toward making the enterprise realistic was taken in the 1970s. The key notion is deriving models from cognitive theories that, when realized as running computer programs, not only embody the theory but also perform the cognitive functions. A (soundly conceived) model of how a human learns can itself learn, and a model of how a human solves problems can itself solve problems. This operational prop-

erty provides an important link in the chain of inferences from theory to observation, allowing behavioral consequences of complex architectural mechanisms (and combinations of them) to be directly determined. Comprehensive models of the human cognitive architecture have not yet been attempted, but several useful models for substantial sub-domains, such as verbal memory, reading, imagery, and skill acquisition, have been put together. This trend toward integration is fundamental to making basic progress.

Sensory Information Processing

Most of our knowledge of the external world comes to us through either our eyes or ears— vision and speech. Hence, understanding the workings of these systems is a prime scientific problem. It is also critical for technological reasons. Vision is necessary for autonomous robots or similar devices that could simulate human performance in industrial settings or in the exploration of space. Speech is necessary to provide the ultimate natural means of communication between humans and machines.

Visual Perception

The end product of the analysis of a visual scene is subjectively familiar. We recognize the objects present in the environment and their spatial relations to each other and are able to compute distances in a way that permits us to navigate; also, the visual experience leaves a residue that can somehow be revived in the form of visual images, which enter importantly into reasoning about natural phenomena. The very earliest stage of the process leading to these consequences is well understood. Light reflected from the visual scene activates a mosaic of receptor cells on the surface of the retina at the back of the eye. But how information about objects in three-dimensional space is extracted from the two-dimensional mosaic of stimulated points and transmitted through the nervous system over nerves that carry information only by virtue of rates of firing of nerve impulses presents a formidable problem. It is somewhat paradoxical that the retinal image contains an enormous amount of information (for example, an aerial photo is typically digitized into about 70 million bits) yet underdetermines the three-dimensional scene that gave rise to it. Thus a device that could build a representation of a scene in the manner of human vision must incorporate knowledge other than the momentary visual input. Discovering precisely what knowledge will suffice and what computation must be performed on the input to yield a three-dimensional representation is a prime task for cognitive science.

The early stages of visual processing produce representations of basic information, such as contours, texture, motion, and depth, that provide the basis for determining shape. All these pose very hard scientific problems, both to discover what the mammalian visual systems do and to produce computational systems with equivalent performance. On none of these aspects are we close to attaining human levels of performance. This is not for want of practical incentive; high-quality systems for any of these would be extremely useful in artificial vision systems and would feed directly into the development of robotics. Indeed, substantial artificial intelligence research has already occurred on them all.

The current lead problem of this kind is that of stereo vision, namely determining just how the brain combines the images of a visual scene coming from the two eyes and uses small differences between them to construct a representation of the scene in depth. However, each image contains a very large number of elements, and it is a most difficult problem to construct search algorithms to find the element of one image that corresponds to any given element of the other. Some progress has been achieved by what are termed relaxation methods, but stereo algorithms take inordinately long to run on available computers. Recent developments in computer hardware technology, using very large scale integrated circuits, now provide the opportunity for significant advance. Using very large numbers of parallel computations, the three-dimensional field can be generated efficiently from the two-dimensional mosaic of retinal receptor elements. There are high hopes that in the next few years this problem will be solved, and we will obtain computational performance in the realm of human performance. This would represent a signal achievement, opening the way to an assault on the other problems of this type.

Because the exploration of low-level vision algorithms is being driven by what we know about psychophysics and neuroscience, this is the area in which cognitive science and artificial intelligence are in closest touch with neuroscience and where the prospects for a highly profitable bridge are best.

Speech Recognition

Since the 1950s, recognizing speech has been a prime target both of speech scientists and of technologists trying to develop recognition machines that would enable easy communication between human and computer. Speech recognition might seem a simpler problem than vision because its input is only one dimensional, not two, but speech has additional complications stemming from the complex encoding produced by the vocal apparatus. What appears to the native listener as a discrete sequence of words is, viewed acoustically, a continuous signal without breaks. Each small sound interval is the result of several contiguous segments of the speech it purports to represent—posing a genuine decoding task. Much of the progress to date has come only with the drastic simplification to recognizing separated words rather than continuous speech—the current commercial market is built upon this reduction. The recognition of words in normal continuous speech remains a major open problem.

In speech, as in vision, ambiguity of perception can be resolved by using knowledge and search heuristics from the cognitive realm. Efforts to bring these resources to bear on continuous-speech recognition programs in the 1970s yielded substantial progress—but only to the point of handling limited vocabularies (1000 words) in systems with strong syntactic and semantic constraints. Recent empirical work, however, has demonstrated that human listeners can recognize continuous speech efficiently using only low-level knowledge of words and phonology, together with knowledge of how basic speech sounds are realized in the acoustic wave form. Implementing these results in artificial intelligence programs offers promise of a new burst of progress.

Natural Language

The understanding of natural language has come to be one of the central problems of cognitive science. (By *natural language*, we mean language as learned and used in ordinary life, as distinguished from the formal languages of mathematics and computing.) One reason is the important role of language in human thought and communication, another the need for machine comprehension and generation of language in order to permit easy and effective communication of humans with computers.

Learning Natural Language

In dramatic contrast with the difficulty of constructing a computer program to understand unrestricted natural language is the speed and apparent ease with which young children learn to cope with language. Preschool children outperform any artificial intelligence program, and the average six-year-old builds new vocabulary at a rate of more than 500 words per month, at the same time perfecting, at an automatic and unconscious level, mastery of a complex of grammatical

rules that enable comprehension and production of an infinite variety of sentences. Moreover, language comprehension requires a semantic analysis of the message conveyed by the language, and learning new concepts often parallels the acquisition of linguistic descriptions for these concepts.

Before we can expect to cope with the full complexity of this learning process, we must accomplish the more basic tasks of investigating the induction mechanisms and knowledge organization principles that give rise to human learning. Significant recent results on learnability, together with some new developments in linguistics having to do with lexically based grammars and their incorporation in models of syntactic processing, are beginning to yield an idea of some of the properties of a reasonable theory of language acquisition. However, the investigation of learning methods is an endeavor that transcends natural language to encompass the acquisition of new skills, concepts, inference rules, and knowledge representations.

Understanding Natural Language

Investigating how adult human beings (or machines) comprehend and produce natural language need not wait on the development of a theory of language learning—and, in fact, has progressed faster. Such research bears on the possibility of easy communication with machines via typed or spoken commands and on the way information is gained from text or discourse in education learning.

The study of natural language understanding can be viewed from three mutually supportive objectives:

1. The identification of linguistic universals and the codification of grammatical systems into principled theories providing a formal characterization of language. This objective is associated primarily with the field of linguistics but clearly affects the automatization of lan-

guage comprehension by computers and the understanding of possible mechanisms that may underlie human communicative abilities.

2. The simulation of human linguistic performance with a view toward understanding human communication, the cognitive processes that support linguistic communication, and the inference system required to extract the intended meaning from the language. This approach is typically associated with cognitive science, and it affects the design and construction of practical language communication systems in major ways.

3. The development of computer systems that can interpret language in limited but increasingly sophisticated domains. This objective is the central artificial intelligence concern with natural language—making computers able to communicate with humans untrained in the intricacies of any particular formal language.

Natural language understanding systems produce internal representations of the information conveyed by the system. The most useful internal representations are *canonical* (recognizing that there are many different ways of expressing the same thought in any language), *semantically rich* (encoding information inferred as well as information explicitly found in the surface form), and *unambiguous* (unlike the natural language itself). These international representations are then applied to a variety of tasks such as text comprehension, data-base query, command interfaces, story interpretation, etc.

Artificial intelligence systems have gradually expanded the capabilities for language comprehension by machine:

- *Lunar* was one of the first truly integrated systems that performed grammatical analysis and subsequent semantic interpretation to answer questions posed by geologists about rock samples obtained from the

Apollo-ll mission. (For example, "What is the average concentration of aluminum in the high alkali samples?")

- *Lifer/Ladder* was the first semipractical system used in data-base query. The final version allowed some tolerance for user errors such as misspellings or the use of occasional sentence fragments.

- *Margie*, *Eli*, *Sam*, *Pam*, and *Politics* were based on a scheme of encoding semantic relations called conceptual dependency. Rather than striving to provide user interfaces, these systems attempted to emulate human comprehension and focused on performing inferences about the intents, plans, and possible outcomes of the speaker in a dialog or of characters in stories. This work demonstrated how language comprehension is an integral component of the total human cognition rather than a separable skill. The same mechanisms used for solving problems, planning actions, and recognizing situations come to play in interpreting and generating language.

Additionally, theoretical work in the structure of dialogs, such as speech-act theory, dialog focus, and belief spaces, has paralleled the implementation of working-language interpreters. Moreover, recent advances in linguistics, such as Lexical Functional Grammar, are unifying previous purely syntactic approaches (such as Chomsky's transformational grammar) with semantic interpretation methods. These parallel theoretical developments, together with recent work on robust parsing (i.e., understanding ungrammatical language) and advances in generating language from conceptual structures, promise to yield a new generation of more flexible and powerful language understanding systems. Such systems are starting to be prototyped as unified practical language interfaces to expert systems, data bases, operating systems, and other computational facilities.

Neither the artificial systems nor the models of human comprehension yet come close to a satisfactory treatment of full language understanding. Nonetheless, this area is one in which returns for investment in research are sharply on the upswing.

INTELLIGENT SYSTEMS

The recent highly publicized advances in artificial intelligence in developing so-called expert systems reflect progress in understanding how substantial knowledge can be used to perform tasks. They have used realistic tasks, such as medical diagnosis, petroleum prospecting, and industrial assembly, and enough highly specific knowledge to almost entirely eliminate search. For example, *Mycin*, one of the classical expert systems, performs diagnosis for particular realms of bacterial infections (e.g., blood diseases) and does so at the level of a medical expert. *Mycin* is a collection of several hundred rules, each of which expresses a bit of diagnostic knowledge and each of which actively calls itself forth whenever it is relevant to advancing the diagnostic task. Each rule is applicable to only a few situations, but in the aggregate they provide a mosaic of coverage that produces, in effect, a field of responses that guides the program in all situations. This knowledge, extracted from expert physicians, represents codified know-how. Though strands of medical science weave through it, just as in all clinical medicine, it is really the accumulated wisdom-applied-to-action of the experts, not their ability to reason or understand.

Systems with Full Expertise

The progress into programming with lots of knowledge, rather than with lots of search (or with highly repetitive algorithms, as in scientific computation), although it has already opened up interesting domains of application, simply sets the stage for the next round of important research. One immediate issue, for instance, is how to weld together extensive knowledge and extensive search in a single system in which the spaces of possibilities to be searched can be created and evoked wherever appropriate.

Another major issue is how to provide such knowledge-intensive programs with a deeper understanding of the substantive domain of their expertise, so they can reason their way to conclusions and can explain why its advice is sound. (Present systems do provide some explanation, but it is relatively shallow, in accord with the superficial character of their knowledge; for instance, *Mycin* can present the rules used in a particular diagnosis to explain what it did.) A substantial body of active research on the nature of such basic understanding is concerned with examining how human experts understand their domains of expertise. The cognitive science research into the nature of expertise is in close contact with the more applied work on expert systems being pursued within artificial intelligence. As a result, we expect the current rather shallow expert systems to metamorphose into much more capable systems—and more scientifically satisfying examples of intelligent agents.

Learning

Studying simultaneously how intelligent systems work and how they acquire their capabilities is so large a task that over their early decades both artificial intelligence and cognitive science resorted to fractionation. In each case the first focus of effort was on the static aspects of information processing.

Artificial intelligence has so far made its major gains by concentrating on performance—on what is needed by way of representation, however, and search to accomplish tasks of varying degrees of difficulty and specification. Nonetheless, the problem of learning is a bottleneck for both practical and theoretical reasons. Expert systems with millions of knowledge rules can be generated only by learning, and in truly intelligent systems learning must go on concomitantly with all problem solving. So until learning is understood, we are walking on one leg. Sparked by these needs, and a better grasp of the theoretical and computational tools required to approach the problem, a resurgence of work on learning is under way.

In cognitive science we have just come through a period in which attention has been focused almost exclusively on the end products of learning—the way acquired information is represented and organized in memory. With some significant results in hand, we are seeing a better balance, with the emergence of studies in concept learning and skill learning. The former line is elucidating how people learn both formal and natural categories (for example, logical or mathematical as compared to biological categories or colors). In the latter line, new experimental approaches in conjunction with models are yielding insight into the way extremely high levels of skill are attained in some areas (for example, the performance of mnemonists and "lightning calculators").

The increasingly close intertwining of the artificial intelligence and cognitive science approaches raises prospects of significant advances in our understanding of learning in all of its various guises. The results can be expected to spill over to the full field of artificial intelligence, as learning mechanisms are incorporated into performance programs in myriad ways, and should amplify the applicability of cognitive science to problems of education.

SCIENCE AND MATHEMATICS EDUCATION

Educating people in technical subjects is a good example of how work from many parts of cognitive science and artificial intelligence comes together. It is both a currently active area of research that shows great promise for making fundamental advances and an area that is capable of making solid contributions to the nation's education problems. Current distress with early science and mathematics education is due in part to social and economic factors but also in part to aspects of

learning and instruction where contributions might be sought from cognitive research and theory. The issues and potential contributions are somewhat different in two major problem areas.

Tutorial Systems

One of the roots of difficulties at higher levels of education is generally believed to lie in our continuing inability to produce acceptable skill at reading, spelling, elementary arithmetic, and the like in the full population of normal school children. A similar problem is becoming acute in the training or retraining of adults in the basic knowledge and skills needed for employment in jobs with increasingly high technical demands.

From the standpoint of cognitive theory, what might be a source of our persisting lack of success at producing basic skills in the full population of normal school children? A firm generalization arising from research on learning of skills is that acquiring significant competence in domains of any difficulty requires large amounts of guided practice—much more than is provided for most pupils in schools or most adults who try to prepare for new technical jobs.

The combination of advances in cognitive theory and basic advances in computer technology (providing interactive workstations of substantial power at increasingly modest costs) makes possible significant inroads into the problems posed by technical education. What can be expected of computer-implemented instruction at this juncture? An intelligent tutoring system that can provide genuine help in educating a student in some well-understood domain, such as mathematics or science, must provide several components.

1. A powerful model of the task domain, so it can itself solve problems in that domain.
2. A detailed model of the student's cur-

rent level of competence, encompassing both partial and erroneous competence as well as perfect competence.

3. Principles for interpreting the student's behavior, so as to be able to infer the student's knowledge and difficulties.
4. Principles for interacting with the student, so as to lead the student to a higher level of competence.

Experimental tutoring systems already exist for significant aspects of geometry, algebra, and arithmetic, and others are currently under development for some aspects of computer programming and elementary physics. For instance, a system dubbed *Euclid* works with a student who is learning to prove theorems in geometry—querying the student, evaluating progress, and providing advice.

The work in tutoring also feeds back and contributes to basic understanding of cognitive science and artificial intelligence. Recall *Mycin*, the artificial intelligence expert system mentioned earlier. The *Mycin* analysis of its task domain of diagnosis made it a candidate for an automated tutor capable of instructing medical students. An attempt to construct such an intelligent tutor showed that *Mycin*'s knowledge was too purely diagnostic know-how and that *Mycin*'s problem-solving style was too different from appropriate human strategies. A revision of the *Mycin* system (called *Neomycin*) attempts to provide a much more cognitively relevant treatment of the task, thus leading back to relevant research on the expert system side.

As artificial intelligence provides expert systems in an increasingly wide variety of tasks, and as the models of students' performance and learning proliferate, the potential exists in this area for a substantial contribution to education in science, mathematics, and technology. Additional elements not yet technically feasible, such as natural language interaction, should soon become possible. Progress on natural language interfaces for tutoring systems is expected to move at a more rapid pace than general research on language comprehension because the constrained nature of the domains to be taught allows simpler, though less general, techniques to be used.

Mental Models and the Problem of Transfer

To have an adequate supply of college-age students ready to move toward careers in science or engineering, effective education in mathematics and science must have begun much earlier. But it is a hard fact that these subjects are regarded as difficult, and very large numbers of children, perhaps including some of the most talented, are turned off by their early experiences. Furthermore, results of cognitive research suggest that faulty starts may be very costly. Inappropriate modes of thinking instilled at an early age, or during early experience with new material at any age, can be very difficult to modify later.

When solving problems in their field, experts mentally construct *qualitative* models of their tasks and reason within these models by applying knowledge and search. For example, when trying to solve elementary physics problems, expert physicists reason qualitatively about the situation until it becomes clear what calculations to make. They construct a diagram of the physical situation and reason to the variables that determine the motion. In contrast, naive problem solvers attempt to solve such problems by going directly to reasoning mechanically with the equations.

The ability to do qualitative reasoning goes hand in hand with expertise, but qualitative models per se do not necessarily lead to successful problem solving. The physicist's qualitative models are useful because they are built around the concepts of force and energy. When naive problem solvers try to bring their own expertise from daily life to bear on physics problems, their qualitative models look more like the earlier pre-Newtonian impetus models (a ball shot from a circular pipe continues to curve, although gradually straightening out). These naive theories provide a framework within which novices interpret demonstrations intended to teach them new facts and begin to learn to solve quantitative problems. Unless these informal theories are understood by the teacher and painstakingly supplanted by new habits of qualitative reasoning about natural phenomena, they persist as a barrier to learning. Thus, even after conventional instruction in new physical, or other scientific, concepts, students who do well on textbook examples often prove incapable of applying the laws or formulas they have mastered at a formal level to interpret actual physical events. The proper sequencing of experiences with qualitative and quantitative reasoning is, consequently, a critical aspect of early science and mathematics education.

The difficulty of producing transfer of learning from educational experiences to new problems has been a bugaboo since the earliest days of educational psychology. The first major research results discredited the prevailing idea of "formal discipline," the notion that general memory and problem-solving abilities could be strengthened by such measures as instruction in geometry and the classics. But nothing was left in its place except demonstrations of the extreme specificity of most learning to its original context. (In World War II, prospective aerial gunners were given intensive practice on skeet ranges—the sole discernible result being skill at breaking clay pigeons.)

It has become clear that for materials or tasks of any complexity, certainly including all forms of science and mathematics learning, a key to transfer is conceptual understanding. Important recent advances in cognitive science include empirical methods for assessing a person's qualitative understanding of principles in a domain (e.g., motion of objects on surfaces in kinematics) and characterization of the mental models, akin in many respects to scientific models, that individuals form when learning about causal relations in such domains. One intensive new line of research attacks the problem of just how the mental models and modes of problem representation of the truly expert solver of problems in specific areas of science or engineering differ from those of the less competent. Beyond the immediate objective of attaining theories of competence comparable to those now available in linguistics is the longer-term goal of tracing the developmental path from the mental model of the novice to that of the expert. A by-product of this effort is a principled basis for adaptive competency testing—on-line interpretation of a student's problem-solving efforts that yields an assessment of understanding. The methodology is advancing rapidly and seems capable of extrapolation from simple mathematics to such complex practical tasks as nuclear plant operation.

NEEDS AND OPPORTUNITIES

Realizing the emerging opportunities for important theoretical and practical advances depends on the degree to which some important needs for support are met. Currently, much more support is available to computer science and artificial intelligence than to cognitive science. This imbalance stems directly from their perceived roles as being hard and soft sciences, respectively. Yet it should be clear from this entire report that the two disciplines closely interlock and contribute to each other at every level and on every scientific problem. Cognitive science especially needs resources to permit it to contribute as a full partner.

The situation in basic artificial intelligence research has a different character. Surrounded by the sudden expansion of applied artificial intelligence, with its rash of new venture-capitalized firms and industrial laboratories, it is hard for basic artificial intelligence research to compete for the talented scientists. Even much basic research is seen by those doing it as very close to real application; hence, bright young scientists are tempted to move toward the commercial sector. From a broad social perspective this somewhat frenetic activity is merely the concomitant of obtaining the social payoff from science. But it tends to deplete the next generation of basic science. The only solution we know is the standard one of attempting to make the basic research situation sufficiently attractive to counter the dispersive factors.

Two specific factors have tended to dampen progress and may do so more seriously in the future. One is a shortage of computing power, and the other is a dwindling supply of new talent. These affect both cognitive science and artificial intelligence, although from somewhat different sides, as noted above.

Computers are the laboratories of artificial intelligence research and major components of laboratories in cognitive science. Unfortunately, both new theoretical ideas and new possibilities of application are outrunning the computing power needed to implement them. Many well-trained cognitive psychologists and other behavioral scientists are unable to move into newly active lines of research in cognitive science because they do not have access to the computing power and languages required for the development of theoretically significant systems. Even in the research groups where the most intensive efforts in artificial intelligence are going on, what appear to be significant opportunities for new theoretical advances are having to wait until some way is found to give investigators access to substantially increased computing power.

Two distinct kinds of computing power are needed. One is the networked powerful personal computer capable of substantial list processing. Adequate research environments in artificial intelligence now require essentially one machine per active investigator (which includes a substantial fraction of graduate students). The other kind is special hardware systems or artificial intelligence supercomputers (not to be confused with numerical supercomputers, such as the Cray and Cyber machines). These systems are all experimental at the present time and can be built only in computer engineering environments and often only in cooperation with industry.

A factor that is not yet critical but that might seriously constrict the advance of research within a few years is an insufficient supply of new talent. Theoretically significant research in cognitive science and artificial intelligence requires extensive technical training in mathematics, psychology, and computer science. Young people are unlikely to go through the rigors of this training unless there are prospects for research careers. The dwindling opportunities for faculty appointments in cognitive science at research universities is by no means compensated by the increasing opportunities in industry, for the balance of support for applied versus basic research is quite different in the two cases. If we want many talented young people to embark on the road to expertise in cognitive science, it would need to become known that a commitment to the support of basic research in this area on the part of the government and universities is sufficient to provide reasonable prospects of research careers.

The needs of this field for carefully engineered support are well balanced by the emerging opportunities for significant theoretical and practical advances. A number of promising possibilities are apparent in the research areas surveyed in this report.

1. The development of comprehensive and executable architectures for cognition.
2. The understanding of massively parallel computation, both at the level of computer architecture and at the level of models for cognitive processes.
3. The development of effective programs for computer recognition of visual scenes, language, and speech, drawing on the resources of both artificial intelligence and cognitive science.
4. The research that attempts to bridge the gap between both artificial intelligence and cognitive science and neuroscience.

5. The application of what is being learned about high-level human reasoning and processes of skill and knowledge acquisition to the development of a new level of expert systems in artificial intelligence.
6. The development of computer-based intelligence tutoring systems, which can play an important role in educating and reeducating our people for a high-technology society.

However, we do not wish to place too much weight on specific lines of research. Cognitive science and artificial intelligence differ from various predecessors most importantly in the emphasis on general problems of fundamental theoretical significance. Though a full theory of intelligence is still remote, the insight that both intelligent machines and their human counterparts can be seen as instances of the class of symbol-manipulating systems has yielded some general results and opened the way for more.

Broadly viewed, research in both cognitive science and artificial intelligence is showing that the acquisition and organization of information are basic aspects of intelligence in both humans and machines. A salient and pervasive characteristic of human beings, distinguishing them sharply from lower organisms and special-purpose computers, is a tendency to acquire information that goes far beyond current task demands and to organize the accumulating knowledge so that it can be accessed and used in unforeseeable future problem situations. Building this feature effectively into computer systems can be seen as the next major advance in the power of intelligent systems. Cultivating it during human cognitive development may be a key to materially increasing human problem-solving abilities.

An important offshoot of research on artificial intelligence is its clarification of the problems and its development of methods pertaining to the systematization and codification of the enormous accumulation of knowledge in technical domains. It is coming to be widely believed that information processing will be the heart of the next industrial revolution. (Witness the scale of the Japanese Fifth Generation Computer project, centered on very large scale machines for artificial intelligence.) As occurred earlier for energy and the physical sciences, and later for medicine and the biological sciences, only massive basic research efforts can prepare us to keep up with this fast-moving worldwide development.

But machine intelligence alone will not suffice. Human intelligence must comprehend the emerging problems and the machines that aid in their solution. Thus, new challenges face our already heavily burdened education system. Cognitive science may be able to provide the broadened theoretical framework within which significant progress can occur and artificial intelligence major components of the needed new educational technology.

*Report of the
Research Briefing Panel on
Immunology*

Research Briefing Panel on Immunology

Hugh O'Neill McDevitt (*Chairman*), Stanford University School of Medicine

Barry R. Bloom, Albert Einstein College of Medicine

John J. Farrar, Hoffmann-La Roche, Inc.

C. Garrison Fathman, Stanford University School of Medicine

Mark I. Greene, Harvard Medical School

Leroy E. Hood, California Institute of Technology

Kimishige Ishizaka, The Johns Hopkins University School of Medicine

Richard Lerner, Scripps Clinic and Research Foundation, La Jolla, California

Philippa Marrack, National Jewish Hospital and Research Center, Denver, Colorado

Stuart F. Schlossman, Dana-Farber Cancer Institute, Boston, Massachusetts

Jonathan W. Uhr, The University of Texas Health Science Center at Dallas

Irving Weissman, Stanford University School of Medicine

Staff

C. Garrison Fathan, *Rapporteur*, Stanford University School of Medicine

Barbara Filner, *Associate Director*, Division of Health Sciences Policy, Institute of Medicine

Linda Peugh, *Administrative Secretary*

Talitha A. Shipp, *Secretary*

Gail Wilson, *Secretary*

Allan R. Hoffman, *Executive Director*, Committee on Science, Engineering, and Public Policy

Report of the Research Briefing Panel on Immunology

INTRODUCTION

Four questions have long intrigued immunologists:

1. How does the immune system have the ability (or the potential ability) to construct an antibody to virtually any foreign material—thousands and thousands of distinct foreign molecules, some not even found in nature but constructed in the laboratory?
2. How does the immune system recognize "self" and accept it while rejecting that which is foreign?
3. How does the immune system's memory work (the ability to respond more quickly and more strongly when challenged with a foreign material it has "seen" previously)?
4. How do the several cell types involved in the immune system communicate so that an integrated, regulated response effectively removes foreign material?

In the past two decades, immunologists have gained substantial understanding about the biochemical structure of the antibody molecule and the processes that enable the genetic system to generate such a great diversity of antibodies. They have learned of two major cell types—B cells and T cells—and have inquired deeply into the regulation of functions of the B cell. The T cell has been more elusive. However, recent advances in basic knowledge and some powerful new technologies have created major new scientific opportunities to identify the role of the T cells involved in regulation of immune responses and to understand the surface molecules (receptors) and secreted molecules (lymphocyte hormones) that mediate necessary interactions.

This new knowledge is leading to such a sufficiently clear understanding of the workings of the immune system that it can now be manipulated toward quite precise experimental and clinical goals. We can study the molecular mechanisms not only of the immune response but also of other basic biological processes, particularly those entailing cell interactions mediated by surface molecules or by minute amounts of protein signals.

Such recently acquired knowledge and techniques also have tremendous potential for the improvement of human health, for making possible effective new means of diagnosis, therapy, and disease prevention. In fact, the potential already is moving toward realization at the level of clinical experimentation.

The technological tools that have allowed these opportunities to develop include monoclonal antibodies, cloning of genes, cloning of immunocompetent cells, and automated and highly sensitive sequence analysis and synthesis of nucleic acids and peptides.

The major research opportunities for the near term are the T cell receptor and lymphocyte hormones (lymphokines), both activators and suppressors.

This paper will explain immune responses, the power of the technological tools, and the reasons why the T cell receptor and lymphocyte hormones would be significant and fruitful areas for scientific inquiry. The paper concludes with a discussion of the additional opportunities that would be offered by this new knowledge—opportunities to advance basic knowledge of the immune system, its responses and regulation of those responses; opportunities to advance knowledge of other basic biological processes and of disease processes; and opportunities to exploit this knowledge with new approaches to the prevention, diagnosis, and treatment of an array of diseases, such as autoimmune disorders, cancer, genetic disorders of blood, infectious diseases, and virtually any health problem for which organ transplantation offers a solution.

IMMUNE RESPONSES

When the body is challenged by a foreign substance (antigen) that is extracellular, such as bacteria, certain cells of the immune system respond with proteins (antibodies) that recognize and bind to the antigen. That response, called "humoral immunity," is mediated by B cells, which secrete a large number of antibodies into the blood. The antibodies mobilize many other immune system activities to rid the body of the foreign substance. A different kind of immune response is at work in intracellular infec-

tions, allergic reactions, or rejection of transplanted organs. This entails "cell-mediated immunity," a function of T cells.

Both B and T cells are lymphocytes originating in bone marrow. Each B or T cell recognizes a specific antigen and can synthesize a unique receptor that recognizes the antigen. Upon appropriate contact with the antigen, the B or T cells are stimulated to divide. They produce a "clone" of identical cells; cells in the clone produce identical receptor molecules and thus have identical specificity for antigen.

One of the great research successes of the past two decades has been the answer to the first question we posed: How does the immune system construct unique antibodies against a seemingly infinite array of foreign substances? The determination of the amino acid sequences of the protein chains in antibodies* and parallel genetic studies revealed that part of the immune cell's DNA is rearranged in order to provide the requisite antibody diversity. In other words, genetic endowment is not rigid and the precise structure for each antibody molecule is not inherited. Gene parts are provided, but they are sorted and resorted to form many new combinations.

This surprising discovery opened the door to a truly revolutionary view of all genes—one that encompasses control of expression during growth and development by rearrangement of a portion of DNA from one site to another along the length of a chromosome.

---

*A typical antibody molecule consists of two pairs of protein chains—two identical heavy (long) chains and two identical light (short) chains. Each chain, whether heavy or light, has what are called "constant" regions and "variable" regions. The constant regions are the same for a large number of antibody molecules, even though their specificity varies. This part of an antibody molecule confers properties held in common, such as helping to trigger inflammatory responses. The variable region, which provides specificity for antigens, is what makes each antibody clone unique.

Recent research has shown that this is indeed true for a number of genes, not only those determining antibody structure.

MAJOR TECHNOLOGICAL GAINS

Recombinant DNA technology and relatively stable and homogeneous B cell lines were essential for the advances in knowledge of B cells. With new technology, the time has now arrived to investigate T cells, their receptors, and their regulation. The relevant technological achievements are the production of monoclonal antibodies, the cloning of genes, and the cloning of immunocompetent cells. Advances in sequence analysis and chemical synthesis of nucleic acids and proteins offer additional promise for the future.

MONOCLONAL ANTIBODIES

In 1975, Kohler and Milstein showed that certain malignant mouse cells that produce antibody molecules (myeloma cells) could be fused with normal antibody-producing B cells. The resultant "hybridoma" cells can be grown continuously and indefinitely as cell cultures that synthesize large amounts of antibody molecules. The antibody produced by such a clone of hybridoma cells is called "monoclonal antibody" and has the important property of having a single specificity—all of the antibody molecules are identical.

Because of unlimited possibilities in producing hybridomas, there is the potential to produce antibodies against a seemingly endless variety of important antigens. There is the technical hurdle of finding a clone with the desired specificity for antigen, but considerable ingenuity has been exercised in screening and selecting for clones of interest.

The discovery of hybridomas and monoclonal antibodies launched a new era in immunologic research and in the application of immunologic assays to basic and clinical problems. One research application has been in the identification of T cell types and eluci-dation of their biological functions. Other research applications cross a broad spectrum of biological areas.

CLONING OF GENES

The genetic information specifying the structure of protein molecules, such as enzymes and antibodies, is encoded in a cell's DNA. It is translated into a working copy—messenger RNA—for use by the protein synthesizing apparatus of the cell. Advances in genetic engineering (recombinant DNA technology) have enabled scientists to isolate messenger RNA from cloned cell populations with defined characteristics, such as the synthesis of a particular protein, make a DNA copy of the genetic blueprint inherent in the RNA, and then incorporate that DNA copy into the DNA of a virus. Monoclonal antibodies can then be used to detect those viruses that have "expressed" the protein of interest during their infection and reproduction in appropriate cells. Once the virus and then its DNA are isolated, the gene of interest can be purified.

Thus, by using recombinant DNA technology and monoclonal antibodies, one can isolate in very few steps the genes that encode proteins of biological and clinical interest. Antibody-directed gene cloning should lead to the rapid isolation of almost any gene, provided the researcher can define a functional polypeptide (protein-like molecule) and the cell that produces it. These immunologic and recombinant DNA technologies should continue to produce a rich diversity of reagents for identification and isolation of biological macromolecules of scientific, clinical, and commercial interest.

In particular, gene cloning should enable immunologists to study in detail the function of genes expressed selectively in particular cells of the immune system. Included would be antigen receptors located on the surface of T cells, other receptor systems that govern interactions between lymphocytes and other cells, and the hormones that regulate the growth and differentiation of the immune system's cells.

CLONING OF IMMUNOCOMPETENT CELLS

Recent discoveries have made possible three different approaches to the long-term growth of T cell clones in cell culture. One method adapts the hybridoma technique first developed for B cells and fuses malignant T cells with normal T cells. A second approach depends on the addition of "growth factors" to the cell culture medium. A third approach involves repeated stimulation of the cultured T cells with a particular antigen and serial reculturing.

These three approaches have set the stage for the identification and isolation of a variety of cell types and secreted cell products involved in regulatory events mediated by immunocompetent T cells. Preliminary experiments using similar approaches suggest that it will be possible to readily clone other sets of immunocompetent cells, including B cells and antibody-presenting cells. This suggests the eventual possibility of constructing an integrated in vitro network of the cells that govern immune responses.

CHEMICALLY SYNTHESIZED ANTIGENS

Proteins, which consist of long chains of amino acids folded into a three-dimensional structure, trigger immune responses and thus are active as antigens. Certain peptides, which are short chains of amino acids, also can act as antigens. Some chemically synthesized peptides have been found to mimic the relevant structure in natural antigens and to elicit immune responses.

What once took the efforts of several laboratories over a period of years (e.g., determination of the amino acid sequence of a single protein chain) can now be done overnight or in a period of days with automated machinery. The technologies that enable rapid and accurate analysis of the amino acid sequence of proteins and the chemical synthesis of peptides offer opportunities to probe the basis for antigenicity. In more applied terms, these technologies also offer opportunities to produce exceedingly safe new vaccines that completely lack an infectious agent. Chemical synthesis also provides the possibility of tailoring an antigen to be a more potent immunologic stimulant. New vaccines against hepatitis, polio, rabies, and herpes viruses are being designed using this approach.

For the future, there is no reason to restrict research to peptide mimics of antigens. Organic chemicals should be considered as well. If we learn the rules by which proteins can be mimicked by organic compounds, we can think in terms of entirely new classes of drugs. This would have applications not only in vaccine development but also in the treatment of hormone and enzyme disorders.

RECEPTORS AND SIGNALS THAT REGULATE THE IMMUNE SYSTEM

The immune system has two main attributes: recognition of self and nonself and immunologic memory. Both recognition and memory are a function of the receptors on the surfaces of immunologically competent lymphocytes and of the protein products elaborated by such cells.

The receptors on B cells that enable them to recognize and respond to foreign materials have been known for some time. They are immunoglobulin (antibody) molecules, closely related to the antibody molecules these cells secrete after stimulation. The protein structure of these molecules and the genes encoding them have been among the most rewarding areas of immunologic research in recent years.

THE T CELL RECEPTOR

Characterization of the antigen-specific receptors on T cells has been elusive. There are two major reasons for the difficulty: (1) T cells, unlike B cells, do not secrete soluble receptor materials, and (2) the receptors on T cells bind only to antigen when it is associated with proteins on the cell surface membrane, not to free antigen. This second phenomenon, identified by pioneering work in the mid-1970s, has been termed "restricted recognition." The cell membrane proteins involved in T cell recognition are the products of a collection of genes that constitute a locus called the major histocompatibility complex (MHC). Restricted recognition of antigen by the T cell suggests that its responses will be directed only at cell-surface-associated antigens. A cytotoxic T cell, for example, will kill a virus-infected cell that bears virus antigens and MHC products on its surface but will not interact with circulating free virus. (Free virus will be removed by antibody that is the cell-free product of B cells.)

For the immunologist the property of restricted recognition makes it difficult to describe the nature of the antigen-MHC protein complex recognized by T cell receptors. Indeed, it is still not known whether the T cell has two different types of receptors, one for antigen and one for MHC, or a single receptor that recognizes some sort of aggregate of the two molecules. The phenomenon of restricted recognition means that binding to antigen or to MHC cannot be used as an enrichment technique for the isolation of T cell receptors for a particular antigen. The situation has prevented our understanding how one-half of the immune system (T cells) recognizes antigen and regulates the function of the other half (B cells).

Two of the new techniques outlined above, however, have contributed to the recent isolation of T cell receptors for antigen-plus-MHC by several laboratories. One technique depends on B cell hybridomas; the other employs cloned T cell lines or T cell hybridomas with receptors of a single specificity for antigen-plus-MHC. Several laboratories have shown that mice immunized with cloned T cell lines or hybridomas produce antibodies that either block or mimic recognition of antigen-plus-MHC by these T cell lines. In every case

published to date, the antibodies are specific for the immunizing clone and do not interfere with antigen-plus-MHC recognition by other T cell clones, even those with similar specificities. Apparently it is the variable portion of the T cell receptor that is being recognized by the relevant antibodies.

The discovery of the T cell receptor for antigen-plus-MHC is so recent—and so much remains to be done—that it is difficult to predict exactly what advances will be realized. Certainly it will lead to the isolation and understanding of the genes encoding these products and to knowledge of the structure of the antigen-plus-MHC product that the T cell receptor recognizes. Additionally, it is known that certain cell surface molecules are associated with T cell receptors for antigen-plus-MHC and contribute to the overall interaction between T cells and their targets. These molecules—LFA-1, OKT4, and OKT8—may have genetic variants that affect their function. Isolation of these molecules and receptors will enable us to understand their function and perhaps to control their action.

Basic understanding of some disease processes also can be foreseen as possible extensions of this research. Many inherited diseases in humans are genetically linked to the MHC, including some so-called autoimmune diseases, such as juvenile-onset diabetes, rheumatoid arthritis, and multiple sclerosis. Because recognition of antigens by T cells is associated with recognition of MHC products, it is thought that diseases of this type are caused by some sort of abnormal T cell response to antigen-plus-MHC, which leads to cross-reaction with a self-antigen-plus-MHC. Understanding how T cell receptors recognize antigen-plus-MHC should lead to clarification of autoimmune phenomena and perhaps to development of methods of circumventing them.

Additional potential therapeutic applications can be envisioned. If the structure of the T cell receptor is known, and monoclonal antibodies can be raised against unique determinants of it, it should be possible to delete selected clones of T cells. For example, such techniques could eliminate clones of leukemic T cells or cells involved in organ graft rejection. Such an approach has the advantage of leaving the rest of a patient's immune system intact.

LYMPHOCYTE HORMONES

The recent discovery of a new class of molecules elaborated by lymphocytes has led to new developments in understanding cell regulation in the control of immunity. Under the proper stimulus, lymphocytes can produce molecules that stimulate other cell types to divide and replicate. These molecules are called "interleukins," which are a type of lymphocyte hormone. One interleukin active in tumor cells has been defined at the gene level, has been molecularly cloned, and has been shown to promote lymphocyte division. This linkage of immunology to cellular and molecular biology should provide valuable insight into the regulation of cell growth and cell division.

With interleukins, immunologists have been able to undertake cellular cloning of T cells. The clones of T cells grown under the influence of these molecules can now give insight into the molecular organization of the recognition system of these uniquely specific cells. Furthermore, it has been found that clones of lymphocytes obtained from mice exposed to tumors and grown under the influence of interleukin-2 can retard and eradicate a similar tumor in other mice. It is anticipated that such interleukins (of which three distinct types have already been defined) will have application to tumor therapies. Interleukin-3 has been shown to promote the division of certain blood cells, suggesting that their growth may be regulated in part by this type of molecule. It is anticipated that interleukin-3 will facilitate the study of blood production by the body and lead to therapeutic modalities for some blood diseases.

Another area of study relates to the expected discovery of other interleukins whose growth-producing activities are restricted to other cells of discrete lineages. Although discovery of interleukins capable of stimulating activities of lymphocytes and other blood cells is clearly a major advance, it also may be possible to identify new genes or to molecularly alter already defined interleukin genes so as to make their hormone products capable of stimulating preferentially one type of cell whose absence needs to be corrected. Furthermore, these interleukins may help provide insight into signals and activities important in the growth of normal and malignant cells. They also may lead to a new family of pharmaceuticals with broad biological activities.

In contrast to the activities that promote cell growth and activity, another class of lymphocyte hormones that suppress cellular activities has been discovered. One type of lymphocyte, termed suppressor T cells, produces molecules that inhibit the development and expression of immunity. These molecules, which still require extensive biochemical definition, are thought to be polypeptides that operate in a sequence of cellular interactions to inhibit both B cell and T cell immune responses.

Areas of study for suppressor hormones relate primarily to the ways in which suppressor cells become activated by antigens, to the biochemistry of the molecule produced, and to the action of such cellular products in the inhibition of cellular processes. Previous research has been hampered by the very low concentrations of some of the suppressor hormones—insufficient amounts of hormone were available for biochemical and biological analysis. But the detailed study of the structure of suppressor lymphocyte hormones will undoubtedly be facilitated by B and T cell hybridoma technology. If both hybridomas that secrete homogeneous products and monoclonal antibodies for these products are developed, it should be possible to clarify the structure of the hormones. It also will be possible to determine the genes that encode these inhibitory substances and to study their organization.

The further development of human suppressor hybridomas is important. Since allergic diseases are caused by antibodies in a class called IgE, selective suppression of IgE antibody formation would be the fundamental treatment for these diseases. Human T cell hybridomas that produce IgE suppressor factors or that could be used for cloning of genes controlling such factors would provide a new strategy to control allergic diseases. Human hybridomas capable of elaborating nonspecific suppressor molecules have recently been defined. Thus, the development of more specific human suppressor hybridomas may have therapeutic application to transplantation and inflammation in addition to allergic responses.

Some mouse hybridomas secrete specific substances that inhibit inflammatory responses similar to those that occur in many pathological states of human beings. The development of human suppressor substances may prove useful in the treatment of autoimmune, allergic, and connective tissue disorders, in which abnormal humoral and cellular responses contribute to morbidity.

Suppressor cells may inhibit myeloma growth, suggesting that lymphoid dysplasias may benefit from new types of suppressive therapy. However, in other solid tumor models, suppressor cells can become activated and inhibit eradication of tumors. Thus, it is likely that another area of development will include strategies to bypass or regulate suppressor activity, which could lead to therapies for human cancers.

APPLICATIONS OF NEW IMMUNOLOGIC KNOWLEDGE

These advances in knowledge of the immune system will play a crucial role in furthering our understanding of basic biological processes and will have medical applications as well. The basic biological processes stud-ied certainly will include the mechanisms and control of immune responses but also will include virtually any biological process involving cell-surface alterations, cell-surface interactions, or cellular communication via peptides present in very low concentrations. We have indicated already the additional important applications to basic research involving isolation of genes.

BASIC RESEARCH

Over the next decade there will be a rapid accumulation of antibodies reactive with many cell types and cell products. Already there are monoclonal antibodies that distinguish the two major classes of lymphocytes in the immune system, T and B cells, and that recognize subsets of these cells specialized to perform different functions. Antibodies will be developed to react with the new lymphocyte hormones and their receptors on the target cells. The ability to distinguish the multiple cell types and cell products participating in immune responses will help to elucidate the systems that control these responses.

It is likely that monoclonal antibodies will be generated that react with cells of many organ systems and even with subsets of cells in those organ systems. These monoclonal antibodies to various cell-surface antigens would constitute a library of molecules that distinguish cells in a precise way that was hitherto impossible. It is expected that the surface antigens will help identify different phases of function, different stages of maturation, or different lineages of differentiation. This identification will help elucidate the processes involved in control of diverse biological processes.

MEDICAL APPLICATIONS

The potential diagnostic, therapeutic, and preventive applications of this new knowledge in immunology are too numerous to discuss here in detail. New approaches are apparent for autoimmune diseases, cancer, and genetic defects in the blood-forming system, for example. Management of infectious diseases, especially via vaccines, and virtually any disorder necessitating organ transplantation also will benefit.

Examples of the readily foreseeable medical uses of monoclonal antibodies, lymphocyte hormones, and recombinant DNA technology are provided by juvenile-onset (insulin-dependent) diabetes mellitus and cancer.

Juvenile-Onset Diabetes

This disease affects 0.5 percent of all children in the United States. It leads to lifelong dependency on injected insulin and to a number of severe long-term complications. Recent research indicates that juvenile-onset diabetes is due to an autoimmune response— antibodies against their own insulin-producing cells are made and the cells are destroyed. It is possible to detect an autoimmune response months or even years before actual development of clinical diabetes.

We already know that most children with this disorder have two particular transplantation antigen types, DR3 and DR4. However, screening is not yet feasible because fully 35 percent of the normal population has these two antigen types. Further biochemical and molecular genetic analysis should identify subtypes that would enable prospective identification of a much smaller population at risk. Screening would then be feasible.

Isolation of the target molecules on the insulin-producing cells would open the way to specifically suppressing this autoimmune response. Use of this target molecule or of human monoclonal antibodies directed against the transplantation antigens involved in the development of autoimmunity might permit therapy that suppresses the autoimmune responses.

Thus, it should be possible within a few years to identify in advance a relatively small percentage of the population at risk for this disorder. These children would be tested on a regular basis for development of the autoimmune response, and treatment to prevent the development of diabetes could be initiated after early signs of autoimmunity.

In the case of juvenile-onset diabetes, monoclonal antibodies seem to offer the best opportunity for identifying, treating, and understanding this autoimmune disorder. For other autoimmune diseases in which there is too much or too little of a lymphocyte hormone, hormone analogs or purified hormones offer possibilities of restoring normal immune regulation.

Cancer

Monoclonal antibodies that are completely pure, have a single specificity, and show high affinity should aid in the discovery of tumor-associated antigens. Antibodies to these antigens offer opportunities for diagnosing tumors that are not precisely identifiable by conventional techniques and could even become the basis for new cancer taxonomies. These antibodies could be used to stain frozen sections, to stain cells dissociated from biopsy material, for tumor imaging, and to analyze blood using flow cytometry. Monoclonal antibodies to tumor-associated antigens also could be used to develop very sensitive radioimmunoassays that will detect these antigens in various body fluids.

One of the major problems will be to determine the distribution of any tumor-associated antigens on normal tissues. If the antigens are not unique to a given tumor, it may nonetheless be possible to use a panel of monoclonal antibodies tailored to assay for particular cancers. The results should allow earlier and more accurate diagnoses.

Monoclonal antibodies also offer new approaches to cancer treatment. They could be used for direct antitumor activity or for targeting delivery of toxic chemicals to tumor cells. For example, there are many highly toxic proteins produced by bacteria or plants—the plant product ricin, for example. A single molecule is sufficient to inactivate protein synthesis and to cause death of the cell in which it is present. Experimental studies indicate that toxins coupled to a tumor-reactive antibody are highly useful in ridding bone marrow of tumor cells. (In the autologous bone marrow rescue approach to the treatment of cancer, the patient's own "cleansed" marrow is transplanted back after massive doses of antineoplastic drugs or irradiation to kill tumors.)

The importance of bone marrow transplantation must be emphasized. In addition to therapy for certain cancers, it is the most obvious means for gene replacement therapy. In genetic deficiency diseases, especially those involving blood cell abnormalities, specific genes could be transferred into bone marrow stem cells, which would then reconstitute the normal functions of the recipient. But even when the donor and host are matched at the major histocompatibility complex, graft versus host disease has a rather high mortality, and this has impeded significantly the use of bone marrow transplantation. Fortunately, animal experiments and preliminary clinical trials indicate that antibody-conjugated toxins directed aginst T cells are capable of "cleansing" bone marrow of those cells that are responsible for the graft versus host disease.

Infectious Diseases

We close this discussion of medical applications with a brief mention of infectious diseases. Recent developments make it possible to purify antigens to an unprecedented extent for use as vaccines. Several methods are feasible, including using monoclonal antibodies to help isolate and purify antigens from natural sources. (One procedure often produces a 5000-fold enrichment in a single step.) Monoclonal antibodies and recombinant DNA technology also allow the genetic engineer-ing of vaccines, and chemical synthesis is possible as well. Yet another approach entails antibodies made against the active site of a specific antibody. Occasionally the anti-antibody mimics the antigenic structure that elicited the specific antibody and engenders an immune response.

An example in which these techniques have been spectacularly effective is the production of a vaccine against the infectious form of the malaria parasite. The sporozoite can be obtained only from the salivary gland of mosquitoes, which do not lend themselves to vaccine production. However, a protective antigen was identified by a monoclonal antibody, the genes of the parasite were cloned in *E. coli*, and recombinant clones expressing the malaria-specific protective antigens were prepared. The vaccine has been found to protect experimental animals.

GROWTH OF IMMUNOLOGY RESEARCH

The truly impressive accomplishments in this field were made possible by the previous national investment of research resources. Vigorous growth in the past five years can be seen in a number of measures. For example, between 1977 and 1981 investigator-initiated research grant applications (ROl) increased more rapidly in immunology than in other fields of biomedical research without compromising quality. (There was a 27 percent increase in the number of competing proposals reviewed by the four immunology study sections of the National Institutes of Health but only an 18 percent increase in other fields.) Furthermore, between 1977 and 1982 the number of new PhDs in immunology increased steadily each year, rising from 101 to 150. We believe that with adequate research resources the scientific opportunities presented in this briefing paper will sustain continued vigorous growth.

*Report of the
Research Briefing Panel on
Computers in Design and Manufacturing*

Research Briefing Panel on
Computers in Design and Manufacturing

Michael Wozny (*Chairman*), Center for Interactive Computer Graphics, Rensselaer Polytechnic Institute

Thomas Binford, Computer Science Department, Stanford University

Robert Brown, Electro-Optical and Data Systems Group, Hughes Aircraft Company

David Grossman, Automation Research, IBM Corporation

Christoph W. Klomp, Computing Systems, Boeing Commercial Airplane Company

James F. Lardner, Deere and Company

Michel A. Melkanoff, School of Engineering and Applied Science, University of California, Los Angeles

Stuart Miller, Automation Systems Laboratory, General Electric Company

Frank Stoneking, Engineering and Manufacturing Computer Coordination, General Motors Corporation

Arthur R. Thomson, School of Engineering, Cleveland State University

Herbert Voelcker, College of Engineering and Applied Science, The University of Rochester

Staff

George H. Kuper, *Executive Director*, Manufacturing Studies Board

Peter Smeallie, *Staff Officer*

Delphine D. Glaze, *Administrative Secretary*

Frances M. Shaw, *Secretary*

Courtland Lewis, *Rapporteur*, Herndon, Virginia

Allan R. Hoffman, *Executive Director*, Committee on Science, Engineering, and Public Policy

Report of the
Research Briefing Panel on
Computers in Design and Manufacturing

SUMMARY

America's future growth in industrial productivity depends vitally on the health of the nation's research in computers for design and manufacturing. In spite of the impressive apparent growth, the panel notes that the central issue in this field is a pervasive lack of scientific knowledge. Universities have made major contributions in the past 10 years with very limited resources.

The first priority of this field is to build a genuine classical research community through increased government support of basic research. The panel identified the following five key research areas that will significantly impact the field:

- geometric modeling and analysis
- human-computer interface for design and manufacturing
- knowledge-based or expert technology
- information management
- manufacturing and computer devices

The second priority is to build our university educational programs in an effort to strengthen America's technical excellence for the long term.

INTRODUCTION

Although the use of computers in design and manufacturing is relatively new, the rapid growth of computer technology and the promise of improved productivity and quality have drastically changed the way we can design and manufacture products. Clearly, issues associated with the application of computers in the factory workplace transcend technology and impact industrial organization, management, and business strategy. Computers will have a profound impact on the work force at all levels, including managers, professionals, and production workers. This report, however, is limited to technical research opportunities for increasing the use of computers that must be explored if the United States is to maintain a competitive edge in design and manufacturing.

RESEARCH GOAL

At the risk of oversimplifying, we can think of design and manufacturing together with marketing as three inseparable parts of a production cycle from conception to delivery. Marketing provides information to engineering and design on the product required.

Engineering designs the product and transfers product-definition data to manufacturing. The planning function within manufacturing transforms the product-definition data, e.g., the geometry, into process-definition data—the instructions for building the product—and then transfers this information to the factory floor. Computer-based planning and control systems directly schedule and track the manufacturing process as well as assure controlling the product's quality with regard to its design specifications.

Research on computers in design and manufacturing should lead to an understanding of the principles necessary to automate completely the creation, analysis, transmission, and management of all product-definition, process-definition, and related business data. This will ultimately take the form of a computer-integrated system. A corollary of this goal is to automate the physical processes corresponding to those data.

Background

University research has contributed significantly to the advancement of this field. For example, the modern concept of computer-aided manufacturing (CAM) had its start in 1949-50 at the Massachusetts Institute of Technology under an Air Force contract. Because of the need to machine aircraft components with complex geometries accurately and reliably, the project led directly to the development of numerically controlled (NC) machine tools. An NC machine uses numeric or symbolic instructions to perform a manufacturing function such as milling or grinding. A subsequent separate effort developed the Automatically Programmed Tool language, called APT, a computer language still used for programming NC machine tools.

During the early 1970s, university research efforts in the U.S. and several other countries created the basis for solid geometric modeling, a complete representation of an object that permits any well-defined geometric property

to be calculated automatically. This concept removed a major roadblock to flexible automation and has tremendous near-term potential to revolutionize the industry. The U.S. university research was funded primarily by the National Science Foundation.

Focus on Mechanical Technologies

There exist two distinct technology areas where computers have been used effectively in design and manufacturing. One technology encompasses microelectronic chip design and fabrication. The other technology is associated with mechanical parts such as machines. Both technologies are very important. Although many of the generic manufacturing concepts, such as planning and scheduling, presented in this report apply to both technologies, the specific research needs for microelectronic design and process modeling are very different from the primarily geometric needs for mechanical design.

This report concentrates on the mechanical technologies because they represent an extremely broad range of diverse manufacturing applications whose mathematical models are not well understood. Mechanical technologies offer significant research opportunities, the results of which will benefit countless small industries. They also represent the fastest growing segment in the field of computer-aided design and computer-aided manufacturing (CAD/CAM).

ASSESSMENT OF THE FIELD

Computers allow us to routinely handle design situations whose complexity is far beyond the reach of an unaided human mind. Furthermore, the level of complexity that can be handled increases with each successive generation of computers.

For example, the computer contributed significantly to the management and design of a modern airplane such as the Boeing 767. The upper or lower wing panel on a Boeing 767 aircraft has stringers attached to it with

18,000 rivets each, the location of which is extremely critical. The wing panel is defined in the CAD/CAM system in a parametric form. More than 1,000 pieces of input information are needed to specify the exact panel location on the wing. Wing panel assembly had been a problem because it was impossible to accurately visualize the results until the stringer was essentially attached, a problem compounded by changes due to engineering error. This entire assembly was completed on the Boeing 767 using CAD/CAM. The computerized assembly allowed visualization of the entire panel prior to engineering release. It also greatly reduced error and improved fit-up so well that on the first panel assembly the actual assembly labor hours required were 72 percent less than originally estimated. In another example, the use of CAD/CAM reduced the time needed to fit the wing joint attachment from two weeks on the Boeing 747 to 18 hours on the Boeing 757.

COMPUTERS IN DESIGN

The computer extends the designer's capability in several ways. First, because the computer organizes and handles time-consuming and repetitive operations, it allows the designer to concentrate on more complex design situations. Second, it allows the designer to analyze complex problems faster and more completely. Finally, the computer allows the designer to share more information sooner with people in the company who need that design information (purchasers, tool and die designers, manufacturing engineers, process planners, etc.). These capabilities result in improved product quality, decreased design-cycle time, and designs virtually impossible to achieve manually.

The following examples illustrate these points. Using CAD, designers at General Motors were able to reduce the total weight of an average automobile by 25 percent and at the same time improve the overall structural integrity of the car. CAD reduced the time required to solve complex stress equations, allowing designers to increase the number of iterations and evaluate more completely the structural changes when metal was removed.

Using computers, GM engineers designing combustion chambers in automotive engines were able to interface a solid geometric model of the combustion chamber to a thermodynamic combustion analysis program, fire the spark, and evaluate how the flame propagates through the chamber geometry. For the first time, a designer was able to evaluate the effect of alternative geometric configurations on combustion without extensive mathematical support to set up the proper boundary conditions. Solid modeling allowed the designers to study analytical problems in a more direct and efficient way than was possible previously.

CAD systems are being used extensively in industry. Although most applications today are in two-dimensional drafting, sophisticated, but limited, three-dimensional surface and solid modeling systems are now on the market. The geometric modeling portions of these systems interface to analysis capabilities by allowing interactive problems to be undertaken. These problems are set up for finite element programs like stress analysis, for kinematics programs like mechanical linkage design, and for NC tool path generation. There is an economic trade-off between two-dimensional and three-dimensional systems, however. Three-dimensional systems require about four times more computer power than the two-dimensional systems. Companies are reluctant to acquire a three-dimensional system because they do not have the trained personnel to use it effectively. Although most CAD vendors are supplying color graphics terminals, their application appears to be for color line drawings rather than the generation of realistic color-shaded images.

Current trends in CAD are toward smaller, more powerful minicomputers. These systems have their own powerful built-in computers for stand-alone operations and can be connected to large mainframe computers for data base access or large analytical needs. Called intelligent workstations, such systems will begin to appear on engineers' desks in the near future.

Research opportunities in CAD are aimed at giving the designer more information about how his or her design will be manufactured. There are many examples in industry where different approaches to the design of the same part lead to different manufacturing procedures with widely varying costs. Future CAD systems will evaluate the merits of a design in progress and offer advice to the designer on the "best way" to proceed. Designers will also be able to access computer models of manufacturing processes for the purpose of evaluating the trade-offs of such contending processes on the manufacturability of the product.

An engineering drawing communicates the designer's ideas and requirements for a part to a machinist. The purpose of a dimension on a typical engineering drawing is to fix some distance or angle used to define an edge or surface of the part. The purpose of the corresponding "tolerance" is to give some acceptable deviation limits on that dimension. Tolerances are necessary because it is impossible to build parts with zero error or precise dimensions. Tolerances influence the machine and tool to be used, the required skill level of the operator, the expected part yield, and many other factors relating to the final cost and performance of the part.

An important step in the design of an assembly is conducting a tolerance "stack-up," or analysis, where potential clearance and interference problems that result from the buildup of tolerances are checked. Assemblies designed using CAD techniques have the advantage of an automated approach to conducting this tolerance analysis.

COMPUTERS IN MANUFACTURING

The major topics in this field are group technology, manufacturing planning and control systems, automated materials handling, computer-aided manufacturing, and robotics.

Group Technology

Group technology is the classification and coding of parts (material, size, shape, volume) and processes (lot size, machine tools, setup time) into families with similar characteristics. It enables the designer to evaluate designs to determine which parts already exist, which parts can be modified from existing parts, and which parts are truly new. Group technology facilitates the establishment of manufacturing cells (groups of machines coordinated to create a given part) for a family of parts, and provides a basis for computer-aided process planning. Direct benefits include a smaller number of parts in inventory (and in the data base), reduced time to design a new product, and increased use of capacity.

Group technology plays an important role in the planning function. Consequently, research is needed to develop models for manufacturing cells or hierarchies of cells that can be used to generate overall optimal scheduling strategies.

Manufacturing Planning and Control Systems

Manufacturing planning and control generally include the following functions: material resource planning (MRP), distribution resource planning, overall simulation and optimization, and shop floor data collection. These functions represent the management and business information needs of the entire enterprise.

The system developed over the last eight years by Ingersoll Milling Machine Company, a large discrete-parts job shop, illustrates the state of the art.* That system

*The company received the 1982 LEAD award (Leadership and Excellence in the Application and Development of Computer-Integrated Manufacturing) from the Computer Automated Systems Association of the Society of Manufacturing Engineers.

integrates a management and business information system with a CAD/CAM system. The system's master scheduler links the bill-of-materials and geometry files to coordinate dispatch, inventory, MRP, planning, and scheduling. High-level management decisions are automatically entered in the system, and each supply source (machine shop, purchasing, stockroom) receives only the appropriate information.

This system has expanded dramatically the existing system's design and implementation capability and provided a major new role in strategic planning. Within four years the productivity of the system's design activity doubled. Today, 82 percent of the system's design time is spent in creative development and only 18 percent on routine maintenance (compared to 42 percent spent in creative development four years old).

The general trend in the area of manufacturing planning and control is toward the integration of more business planning and reporting functions. Although simulation techniques are used extensively to test scheduling scenarios, they cannot yet generate them. An important research problem is the refinement of large-scale optimization techniques to identify planning and scheduling strategies for large, hierarchical, flexible manufacturing systems. Other important topics include inventory management techniques to accomplish ''just-in-time'' objectives and the employment of knowledge-based expert technologies to ensure quality throughout the design, test, and manufacturing cycle.

Automated Materials Handling

The major automated materials handling systems consist of automated storage and retrieval systems, miniloaders, automated guided vehicle systems, and conventional materials/parts storage and transport systems. Benefits include higher inventory record accuracy, reduced storage space requirements, increased labor productivity, and the automatic transmittal of material movement information from the production control system to materials handling equipment.

Computer-Aided Manufacturing

Computer-aided manufacturing generally refers to numerically controlled (NC) machining and other processes (including flexible manufacturing systems), computer-aided inspection and testing, automated assembly, and process control.

In the machining area, NC machines have been used for many years with proven benefits in the form of reduced time for machining and storage. The current trend in the industry is a logical extension of NC to 2 to 15 machine tools linked with automated materials handling and production scheduling—a machining cell. Such systems are commonly used to produce one or more families of parts. Benefits provided by these systems include increased production flexibility, reduced operating costs, and higher machinery utilization.

Computer-aided inspection is an area of intense research. The benefits include automatic collection and analysis of quality control data, creation of data bases to isolate production process problems, and correction of machinery problems before many faulty parts are produced.

A system developed at General Electric Corporate Research and Development for inspecting jet engine turbine blades represents the state of the art. The basic task for that system is to inspect turbine blade surface and subsurface geometry to exacting tolerances at high rates. The inspection system consists of three major subsystems: a subsystem to present and sense the part precisely, a signal-processing and image-processing subsystem to inspect the part, and an analysis and decision-making subsystem to accept or reject the part automatically.

In the electronics area, IBM has developed a robotics-based automated system to test the thousands of connections on the electronic boards of mainframe computers. This system is based on design data that describe the location of the connecting paths.

Automatic assembly systems today are generally built to perform one task. The trend in this area is toward flexible, electronically controlled systems, including assembly robots. It is possible to generate robot programs automatically for well-defined and regular geometric layouts such as circuit boards and cable harnesses.

Model-based CAM has the capability to generate computer programs automatically from geometry and other information, in order to control manufacturing processes and to simulate such processes for verification and evaluation. Automatic procedures would extract pertinent information from underlying models of various processes such as extruding, cutting, forming, casting, welding, painting, hardening, testing, assembly, and material flow. Mathematical bounds on the reliability and optimality of these models are also needed.

In primary processes, such as molding or forming, it is possible to derive mold geometry from part geometry. Modeling mold performance is still largely a research issue.

Logistics models involve material flow and process planning. From a network flow model it is possible to predict assembly-line behavior automatically. However, there is limited ability to derive optimal schedules. It is possible to derive process plans for the sequence of manufacturing steps required for axially symmetric parts.

Research is needed in modeling almost all processes. Models are also needed for sensor-mediated assembly and visual inspection, i.e., the use of sensors to control the process. Such models require better methods of modeling three-dimensional geometry and constraint relationships, including kinematics and tolerances. Methods are needed to permit fabrication planning from three-dimensional geometry.

Robotics

Robotics is an area of intense activity. The major industrial applications include spot welding, materials handling, finishing and coating, arc welding, and assembly. The two most promising application areas for future growth are materials handling, including loading and unloading operations, and assembly.

Current robots can offer very precise and repeatable position control. However, the availability of force sensing, the ability to control the force exerted by the robot's grasping mechanism, is very limited. Virtually no continuous force control is available.

Programming systems are somewhat incompatible with most standard operating systems and programming languages. They also lack features such as coexistence of interpreted and compiled code, configurability, and facilities for debugging, multitasking, multiprocessing, and networking. Smart (adaptive) programming systems are virtually nonexistent.

Current robot vision capabilities are two-dimensional binary and are generally restricted to well-separated parts. Development is under way on applications and systems for structured-light, three-dimensional systems (i.e., systems using light projected in coded form), which will greatly expand the capability.

Given current research, one can expect to see in the next several years general purpose, real-time distributed operating systems and programming languages. Robots will exhibit limited force control, assembly capabilities, and coordinated use of multiple arms. There will also be commercial, structured-light, three-dimensional systems, and limited model-based vision systems.

Methods are needed for linking robots and vision systems to CAM models to allow real-time use of such models. Research is needed on establishing a set of fundamental low-level commands to characterize sensor-mediated actions, such as force-controlled motion.

Integration of the Total System

The total integration of all computer-based systems that support design, manufacturing, and business functions is essential to realize the potential of the computer for increasing productivity. Although significant inroads have been made on a limited scale in specific industries, system integration on a large scale is an extremely complex and poorly understood problem.

The requirements of an integrated system include (1) analytical, operating, and control systems that communicate directly with each other; (2) systems able to generate (by creating, deriving, transforming, and interpreting data) the appropriate information necessary for the support and operation of the design and manufacturing functions; (3) the use of a common data base concept that can be physically distributed over many computers; (4) a responsive communications network; and (5) a master system to manage the whole.

Research is needed to understand the nature of the integration problem. We expect that simulation techniques will be useful in modeling integration concepts to help evaluate the anticipated effects, the reliability, the usefulness (cost/benefit), and the potential likelihood of achieving large-scale integration. Research on this problem is risky because of the comprehensive nature of the changes involved and the enormous investment required. Yet it carries the greatest potential for payoff.

Global Information Structures

We can think of existing research in design and manufacturing as creating the building blocks of a cathedral. We are putting the blocks in place to build the cathedral without actually knowing if the overall structure is going to stand up.

Currently, data carried in traditional industrial data bases is functionally divided to support engineering and manufacturing separately. The engineering data base supports geometry and engineering business data, such as scheduling and purchasing. The manufacturing data base supports the processing aspects of geometry, such as numerical control, and manufacturing business data such as planning and inventory control. In most cases these data are located in several physical data bases.

The data interfaces must be structured to support all the above industrial processes. The structure must be flexible enough to accommodate the information needs for different applications such as machining, scheduling, inventory control, estimating costs, analysis, or design. It is also desirable that the information be derived from the data without human intervention. Yet it must be general enough to permit the integration of current systems and still be extendable to future systems. Such an information structure will in effect become the master source for the definition of both product and process.

The nature of global information structures is not well understood today. Data flow concepts need to be developed and tested against a broad spectrum of applications.

Distributed Data Management and Networking

Applications requiring large data bases and involving different computers in a network create a severe communication problem because most data base management systems run on only one computer. Consequently, data communication problems arise because the data base management system in one computer cannot be used to query data in another computer.

Long-distance data communication between separate geographic sites is another typical problem in heterogeneous computer networks. Current services for the transmission of critical geometric and other data are slow, noisy, and costly. Efforts to establish standards are proceeding but are still unresolved.

Integration of the design and manufacturing of a product can occur only if the heterogeneous software and hardware systems support a common distributed data base. This distributed data base must have adequate recovery and backup procedures when simultaneous updates on different computers occur or when one or more computers in the network fail. It must have minimal redundancy of data while maintaining the most efficient access route and data traffic. Further, it must maintain audit trails of a large variety of simultaneous updates caused by design or manufacturing changes. Research is needed to study the data characteristics necessary to integrate the design and manufacturing systems within a distributed data base environment composed of heterogenous computers.

RESEARCH OPPORTUNITIES

The trends in the application of computers in design and manufacturing identified in the previous section suggest a number of research opportunities. Underlying these areas are a set of generic research topics that can be grouped into the five following areas: (1) modeling, (2) human-computer interface, (3) expert systems, (4) information management, and (5) devices. Research in these areas will provide the critical building blocks needed to speed the application of computers in the factory.

MODELING

Geometric models embody the description of a product design. Consequently, they represent a basic link between CAD and CAM. Most existing CAD systems describe product geometry by means of potentially ambiguous "wireframe" representations, a collection of points and lines. With wireframe representations there is no way of determin-

ing automatically if a point was "inside" or "outside" the object. It is not possible to calculate mass properties (i.e., volume, inertia) in any automatic way. Therefore, automated analysis (and model-driven CAM) will require a complete and unambiguous representation of the geometry in three dimensions.

Geometric Modeling

The ultimate goal of geometry research is to develop a complete and unambiguous three-dimensional geometric representation for part and process modeling. This representation should include free-form (sculpted) surfaces, allow creation of geometry in a natural manner (be user friendly), and permit automatic analysis and process planning.

Current Status The theoretical foundations for computer-based solid geometry representations were laid through university research conducted primarily in the U.S. and U.K. during the 1970s. U.S. industry is just beginning to use solid modeling in production. The solid modelers that are commercially available all have shortcomings.

Industrial research that is focused on methods for improving existing techniques should lead in a few years to solid modelers acceptable to industry with increased capabilities in surface sculpting and blending. Performance should also increase, primarily because of new hardware and improved software.

Key Research Needs An important research problem is the integration of free-form surface generation capabilities into solid modelers. Several approaches currently being investigated appear promising, including the rational B/SPLINE representation and the generation of blending surfaces between a given set of primitive solids. The deformation of solids is another important problem area where very few inroads have been made. The ability to handle deformations, for example, has very important practical implications in modeling the extrusion process. One can identify many such process operations that need to be investigated.

Another research area involves tolerancing information for solids. Current mathematical and computational theories of mechanical tolerancing have significant gaps. Finally, there are many geometry problems such as surface-surface intersection, stable position of free-form solids, numerical accuracy of geometric models, and new geometric primitives that need to be investigated.

Analytic Modeling

There are many analyses needed in the course of a design that involve the creation of an approximate (discretized) geometric model and then the application of loads and material properties. Thermal and stress analyses using finite element techniques are two examples.

Two steps are required to perform these analyses automatically. First, we need an automatic discretization procedure that will provide some type of approximate form of the initial geometric object. Second, we need a way of ensuring beforehand that the numerical results of the analysis will be within a prescribed level of accuracy (adaptive analysis).

Current Status Research is needed in analysis methods that can be applied directly to a geometry configuration with associated boundary conditions in some automatic way. For example, research on automatically generated meshes for finite element analysis is a very active area. Industry-usable results should be forthcoming in the next several years.

Key Research Needs Adaptive analysis is the primary area of needed research. We need the capability of applying an analysis procedure such as stress analysis directly to a geometric model with given boundary conditions and automatically obtaining an answer to a spec-

ified level. This problem has a high research priority because it represents an important step in the automation process. Expert systems are needed to aid the designer in choosing an appropriate approximation model for each condition in the problem (e.g., shell model or beam model for different parts of an airplane).

HUMAN-COMPUTER INTERFACE

The human-computer interface in CAD is the link between a design engineer and the CAD system. A user-friendly interface will guide the designer through complex design tasks in a direct and effective manner. This is very important, especially in the early design decisions that have a major impact on the total design-production process. The development of such an interface requires an understanding of the creative design process. Ideally, the system will act as a natural extension of the designer. Friendly interfaces are especially important in CAM, where users may be less familiar with computing techniques.

Current Status Graphics systems are now very sophisticated, with the ability to create color-shaded, three-dimensional images from a design data base. However, most existing human interface capabilities are still relatively crude with very limited help capabilities to get out of trouble. In short, today's occasional user faces an imposing learning experience each time he or she sits down at the workstation. Graphics and engineering workstation vendors are beginning to pay attention to the relevant human factors and human engineering issues, but the effort is still very limited.

Key Research Needs Research is needed to understand better how an engineer conceptualizes, since it is in the early stages of design that current CAD/CAM is least effective. Modeling cognitive processes associated with design need to be explored. Research is needed in developing "smart" CAD systems that use expert (i.e., knowledge-based) concepts to guide the engineer interactively through a design situation by continually evaluating his or her performance and issuing guidance in terms of the individual's perceived experience base.

Expert Systems

Expert systems consist of a body of knowledge and a mechanism for interpreting this knowledge. The body of knowledge is divided into facts about the problem and heuristics or rules that control the use of knowledge to solve problems in a particular domain.

In the last few years, expert systems have become the most visible and fastest growing branch of artificial intelligence. Their objective is to capture the knowledge of an expert in a particular area, represent it in a modular, expandable structure, and transfer it to other users. To accomplish this goal, it is necessary to address issues of knowledge acquisition, knowledge representation, inference mechanisms, control strategies, user interface, and finally how to deal with uncertainty.

Current Status Expert systems development, confined during the past decade to academic laboratories, is now becoming commercially viable, partly because of the development of well-understood methods for knowledge-based programming and partly because of advances in microelectronics. Current examples of expert systems include MOLGEN, which interactively aids molecular geneticists in planning DNA-manipulation experiments; VM (Ventilator Management), which gives real-time advice for the management of patients undergoing mechanical ventilation in an intensive care unit; PROSPECTOR, which advises when and where to drill for ore; and DELTA, a production rule-based system for diesel electric locomotive repair. Expert systems have not yet been applied in any real sense to solve manufacturing problems.

Key Research Needs Applied research is needed to gain some experience in building knowledge bases for selected manufacturing processes, especially in planning functions. Research is needed to sort out the issues of "design for manufacturability" before undertaking the task of building one. The concept of geometric reasoning is very complex; we need to understand how to characterize manufacturing "reasoning" such as "find a symmetrical object in the data base." Finally, we need to examine closely the issues or experiences involved in developing knowledge bases for making approximations in complex analysis problems.

Information Management

This area concerns the management of design and manufacturing data so that users and systems can use the data easily and efficiently.

A data base is an organized collection of discrete data on a given subject. A data base is made accessible and useful by means of a data base management system (DBMS). This management framework permits users to both query and update the data base in order to derive comprehensive lists of data having certain characteristics in common.

Current Status Data base management systems are commercially available for a wide range of applications. Current research is producing considerable advances in DBMS capabilities, including improved performance, modeling capabilities, and user interfaces. Research on distributed data bases is a critical area. However, there are features of the manufacturing environment that render current data bases and DBMSs inadequate. We do not know how to make data base systems that efficiently handle manufacturing requirements in a distributed environment.

Key Research Needs Research is needed to organize geometric data in a way that allows "geometric reasoning," i.e., to optimize the data extraction operations in response to continually developing and unanticipated user queries. For example, consider requesting a list of parts where the parts possess a certain symmetry, regardless of the sequence of geometric steps used to construct the parts originally. We may not know beforehand that symmetry is important and therefore would not want to assign a symmetry attribute. We want the system to "reason" its way to the correct information.

Other research areas include the following:

- A basic study into the nature of the integration problem. This could lay the groundwork for integrated experimentation on a larger scale.
- The development of data characterization requirements for the integration of systems in a distributed data base environment.
- The investigation of the information structure required to support the so-called neutral data base or master product definition.
- The development of algorithms to support proper recovery and backup procedures of distributed data bases in heterogeneous computer environments.
- The use of simulation techniques to help model integration to understand better the anticipated effects, reliability, usefulness (cost benefits), and the overall potential to achieve actual integration.

DEVICES

This section deals with issues at the device or workstation level as opposed to systems level. The basic technology of robot sensors and actuators must be advanced significantly in order to achieve the needed order-of-magnitude improvement in precision, speed, and dexterity. Component modularity involving new micromechanical, electronic substrate-based sensors and controllers is required for the flexibility needed to create unique manufacturing systems. The ability to integrate

and coordinate comprehensive strategies for sensing and control is also very important.

These objectives imply the need for special-purpose computer architectures and VLSI (very large scale integrated) chip technology. Such chips will also be essential for handling the growing computational workload in automated CAD and CAM modeling and analysis operations. Chips for handling specialized geometric constructions, inference interpretations, and analysis processor calculations will dictate requirements for special-purpose microelectronic chips in the near future.

Current Status   Currently, we have a heterogeneous collection of sensors and actuators and no uniform way of integrating these components into a coordinated manufacturing system. For example, vision systems are important not only for robots but also for all kinds of inspection and control functions.

Array processors for special-purpose analysis calculations and display processor chips for graphics are becoming more widely used. They are only the beginning of a trend toward fast hardware.

Key Research Needs   Research is needed to develop smart sensors, including visual and tactile sensing. The investigation of modularity issues in sensors and actuators is also important. Finally, the development of requirements for special-purpose processors to implement advanced algorithms in analysis, geometry, expert systems, network communications, and control strategies are needed. The research issues here cut across other fields in a significant way. Collaboration will be required. This research is important because the ultimate precision and speed of our manufacturing will be dependent on the inherent capabilities of these devices.

THE ROLE OF UNIVERSITIES, INDUSTRY, AND GOVERNMENT

Universities, industry, and government traditionally have been the key institutions in manufacturing technology research. Each has its own method of addressing research problems, and each has unique limitations and strengths.

SUPPORT MECHANISMS FOR RESEARCH

In universities, research tends to be small scale in nature, where specific, well-formulated problems are studied in a formal manner. Universities have been reluctant to grapple with the larger problems of integration, partly because of inadequate interdisciplinary knowledge (few faculty trained to address such issues) and because of an uncertainty about the scientific issues. Hardware and facilities are costly—usually beyond the means of a university budget. Even when hardware is donated by industry, the operational costs are substantial. In addition, many graduate students in computer-related fields are attracted by industry, sometimes before completion of their degree program. This effectively limits the formation of a cadre of qualified researchers. Government and other funding for university research in this field is insufficient to develop the critical mass of researchers needed to sustain significant progress.

Industrial companies have generally solved design and manufacturing problems piecemeal, addressing short-term objectives. Broad gaps in basic knowledge are increasingly apparent as computers are applied to factory problems that pose larger and more difficult integration hurdles. Compounding these organizational limitations are some situational problems.

1. It is difficult for industry to articulate its systems' integration problems. The issues vary greatly by company size and markets.
2. Manufacturing equipment is generally tied up for production purposes and unavailable for scientific experimentation.
3. The industrial application of research

findings requires capital and personnel investments over a period of years, with accompanying high costs. Also required are in-house advocates to sell the concept, lead the implementation, and provide a critical mass of management approval.

The federal government has been a major customer for existing CAD/CAM products and for highly specialized, one-of-a-kind systems. This latter role has catapulted key government agencies (notably the U.S. Department of Defense and the National Aeronautics and Space Administration) into areas of systems design and management, so that they have become catalysts for advances in knowledge through acquisition, internal research, and sponsored research.

Clearly, our view of these problems is at a point of transition. During the past decade agencies of the federal government have embarked on several programs that have begun to focus attention on both component development needs (the National Bureau of Standards and the U.S. Department of Defense) and system integration problems (the U.S. Air Force and the National Aeronautics and Space Administration). An important factor in these programs is the use of consortia of industrial companies and universities, although university involvement has been limited.

There are a few recent examples of university/industry collaboration at schools such as Rensselaer Polytechnic Institute, Carnegie-Mellon University, and Stanford University. Other universities are attempting to develop similar collaborative efforts, many of them in local areas. It appears that an effective way to conduct research and transfer technology in certain areas would be via these consortia.

Over the years, individual companies have supported applied and generic research at universities through grants of money and equipment. This activity has now been intensified, the most recent development being IBM's announcement in July 1983 of $10 million to five universities for manufacturing-related curriculum development. This was preceded by a $40 million equipment grant to 20 universities.

Individual companies within industries are beginning to explore the feasibility of creating joint R&D partnerships patterned after Microelectronics and Computer Technology Corporation, which was created within the electronics industry to undertake the study of generic research issues.

The central issue in the field of computers in design and manufacturing is a pervasive lack of scientific knowledge. This lack of knowledge is less pervasive than it was 10 years ago, in part because university research has been able to make some significant accomplishments with very limited resources. However, major gaps still exist, as this report illustrates. The first priority of this field is to build a genuine, classical research community. The large integration efforts identified in this report will require a much stronger base of fundamental knowledge than is now available.

EDUCATION AND TECHNOLOGY TRANSFER

As important as the development of technology is the transfer of that technology to an educated work force (including engineers, managers, and operators). There are four basic issues, each requiring a different mechanism. The first issue is the transfer of prototype technology from R&D laboratories to industrial use. University-industry consortia can facilitate this transfer, as will the traditional mechanisms of conferences, publications and product sales.

The second problem is to educate a new breed of engineers who thoroughly understand all aspects of computer-integrated manufacturing (CIM) engineering in its broadest sense. This involves developing new courses and programs and implies a knowledgeable faculty.

The third issue is the integration of modern computing tools into the traditional program of engineering education. These students will become the users (not developers) of CIM.

The last issue is the training of operators and technicians in an effort to upgrade the existing work force. It is necessary to find cost-effective ways of training people at a significantly faster rate and to develop a means of transferring experience without incurring the high cost of one-on-one instruction. Better productivity in training for skill development is a critical need.

*Report of the
Research Briefing Panel on
Selected Opportunities in Chemistry*

Research Briefing Panel on Selected Opportunities in Chemistry

George C. Pimentel (*Chairman*), University of California, Berkeley

Allen J. Bard, University of Texas

John H. Birely, Los Alamos National Laboratory

Michel Boudart, Stanford University

Ronald Breslow, Columbia University

Harry B. Gray, California Institute of Technology

Ralph Hirschmann, Merck Sharp & Dohme Research Laboratories

Alan Schriesheim, Exxon Research & Engineering Company

Howard E. Simmons, E. I. du Pont de Nemours & Company

Barry M. Trost, University of Wisconsin

George M. Whitesides, Harvard University

In cooperation with the NRC Committee to Survey the Chemical Sciences and the Board on Chemical Sciences and Technology

Staff

William Spindel, *Executive Secretary*, Board on Chemical Science and Technology (BCST)

Mary E. Bundy, *Administrative Associate*, BCST

Peggy J. Posey, *Staff Associate*, BCST

Robert M. Simon, *Rapporteur*

Allan R. Hoffman, *Executive Director*, Committee on Science, Engineering, and Public Policy

Table of Contents

Report of the
Research Briefing Panel on
Selected Opportunities in Chemistry

EXECUTIVE SUMMARY

This is a time of special opportunity for intellectual advance in chemistry. It derives from our developing ability to probe and understand the elemental steps of chemical change and, at the same time, to deal with extreme molecular complexity. Powerful instrumental techniques are the crucial dimension. They account for the recent acceleration of progress that gives chemistry unusual promise for high return from additional resources.

Chemistry is a central science that provides fundamental understanding needed to deal with most societal needs: to feed the world population, to tap new sources of energy, to clothe and house humankind, to provide renewable substitutes for dwindling or scarce materials, to improve health and conquer disease, to add to our national security, and to monitor and protect our environment. Further, there can be no doubt that chemistry, with its current $12 billion positive balance of trade, is a crucial element in this nation's economic well-being. Our future international competitiveness will depend upon maintaining our present leadership position in the chemical sciences.

Directions of particular promise are becoming apparent in the course of the NAS/NRC study by the Committee to Survey the Chemical Sciences. This Committee is formulating a multi-year program to exploit the richest potentialities in a priority sequence that will maximize return on the needed additional federal investment. We identify here three areas, those that will yield the greatest rewards and furnish the appropriate beginning to this program.

    A.   Understanding Chemical Reactivity
    B.   Chemical Catalysis
    C.   Chemistry of Life Processes

A.   *Understanding Chemical Reactivity*

We propose an initiative to apply the full power of modern instrumental techniques and of chemical theory to the clarification of factors that control the rates of reaction and to the development of new pathways for chemical change.

• *Molecular Dynamics*: to elucidate the entire course of chemical reactions, including the unstable atomic arrangements intervening between reactants and products.

- *Reaction Pathways*: to accelerate our rate of discovery of new reaction paths and new classes of compounds.

A principal objective of this initiative will be to provide the fundamental basis for U.S. leadership in development of new processes, new substances, and new materials.

B. *Chemical Catalysis*

We propose an initiative to apply the techniques of chemistry to obtain a molecular-level understanding of catalysts. Ultimately, new catalyst systems will result that will lay the foundation for the development of new chemical technologies. The program will emphasize research in four areas:

- *Heterogeneous Catalysis*: to apply the powerful new instrumental techniques of surface science to the study of chemistry on the surface of a solid.
- *Homogeneous Catalysis*: to take advantage of recent developments in synthetic chemistry that show promise as new soluble catalysts.
- *Photocatalysis and Electrocatalysis*: to investigate solution chemistry catalytically assisted by electrode processes, with and without absorption of light.
- *Artificial-Enzyme Catalysis*: to couple the chemists' ability to control molecular topography with the biochemists' understandings of natural catalysts so as to generate a new class of artificial enzyme-like catalysts tailored to specific needs.

A principal objective of this initiative will be to provide the fundamental knowledge and creative manpower required for the U.S. to maintain competitive advantage in catalysis-aided technologies.

C. *Chemistry of Life Processes*

We propose an initiative to develop and apply the techniques of chemistry to the solution of molecular-level problems in life processes. Research at this border between chemistry and biology requires individuals broadly competent in both areas, and a special effort must be made to develop such individuals. The program will emphasize the molecular aspects of six areas:

- Enzymology (understanding the molecular interactions responsible for enzymatic activity; production of natural enzymes for use as catalysts in chemical synthesis).
- Immunochemistry (the chemical basis of the immune and allergenic response; use, function, and modification of monoclone antibodies; synthesis of antigens and adjuvants).
- Chemical Endocrinology (synthesis of hormones and hormone analogs, especially those related to polypeptides).
- Neurochemistry (molecular basis of nerve transmission; neurotransmitters; agonist and antagonist chemistry; membrane polarization).
- Membrane Chemistry and Vectorial Chemistry (bioenergetics; active and passive transport).
- Biological Model Studies (host/guest chemistry; semisynthetic enzymes; properties of aqueous solutions; active site modeling).

A principal objective of this initiative will be to accelerate the conversion of qualitative biological information into techniques and substances useful in biotechnologies, in human and animal medicine, and in agriculture.

In the next two decades there will be dramatic changes in our basic understandings of chemical change and our ability to marshal those understandings to deliberate purpose. The program presented here is intended to define a leadership role for the U.S., as these advances are won. The rewards accompanying such leadership are commensurate with the prominent role of chemistry in addressing societal needs, in ameliorating the problems of our technological age, and in sustaining our economic well-being. The costs of falling behind are simply intolerable.

The need for enhanced federal investment in chemical research is rooted in a pattern of funding historically appropriate to a test-tube and bunsen burner era, an era long since eclipsed. The sophistication of a modern chemistry laboratory requires a much more vigorous financial commitment, both in capital investment and in supporting services. Even so, the cost is miniscule compared to the stakes involved; we must nurture a $175 billion industry that maintains a $12 billion positive balance of trade. We must provide it with a full reservoir of fundamental knowledge and we must attract a substantial share of our brightest young scientists to this rewarding task. This program can accomplish these goals.

Report of the
Research Briefing Panel on
Selected Opportunities in Chemistry

I. INTRODUCTION

This is a time of special opportunity for intellectual advance in chemistry. It derives from our developing ability to probe the elemental steps of chemical change and, at the same time, to deal with extreme molecular complexity. Powerful new instrumental techniques are the crucial dimension. They account for the recent acceleration of progress that gives chemistry unusual promise for high return from additional resources.

Chemistry is a central science that provides fundamental understanding needed to deal with most societal needs. It is a critical component in Man's attempt to feed the world population, to tap new sources of energy, to clothe and house humankind, to provide renewable substitutes for dwindling or scarce materials, to improve health and conquer disease, to add to our national security, and to monitor and protect our environment. Basic research in chemistry will surely help future generations cope with their evolving needs and unanticipated problems.

Chemistry is also a crucial element in this nation's economic well-being. The U.S. Chemical and Allied Products industry employs over a million people, makes manu-

facturing shipments totaling about $175 billion, and currently displays a $12 billion positive international balance of trade, second highest of all commodity groups. Our competitiveness in a range of international markets depends upon maintaining our present position of leadership in the chemical sciences. There is no area of basic science that offers a more secure investment in the Nation's future.

Thus, rapid advances are possible now in chemistry, advances that will continue to enrich our cultural heritage, that will ultimately respond to human needs, and that will sustain our economic competitiveness. Directions of particular promise have become apparent in the course of the NAS/NRC study by the Committee to Survey the Chemical Sciences. This Committee is formulating a multi-year program to exploit the potentialities in a priority sequence that will maximize return on the needed additional federal investment. We identify here three areas that furnish the appropriate beginning to this program.

A. Understanding Chemical Reactivity
B. Chemical Catalysis
C. Chemistry of Life Processes

II. PRIORITY OPPORTUNITIES

Three priority thrusts are described. The first is connected with opportunities to understand, in the most fundamental sense, chemical reactivity and to control it. The second is to advance our understanding of catalysis in all of its facets. The third will extend to the molecular level our understanding of life processes. These three thrusts are complementary and reinforcing in the sequence given. They have different rationales and distinct budget needs, so they are presented separately.

A. *Understanding Chemical Reactivity*

1. *Program.*

We propose an initiative to apply the full power of modern instrumental techniques (lasers, molecular beams, computers, etc.) and of chemical theory to the clarification of factors that control the course of a chemical reaction and to the development of new pathways for chemical change.

- *Molecular Dynamics*: to elucidate the entire course of chemical reactions, including the unstable atomic arrangements intervening between reactants and products.
- *Reaction Pathways*: to accelerate our rate of discovery of new reaction paths and new classes of compounds.

2. *Objectives.*

- To advance our fundamental understanding of chemical reactivity.
- To attract exceptional young scientists to the frontiers of this understanding.
- To apply this understanding to the development of new types of reaction and new classes of compounds.
- To provide the fundamental basis for U.S. leadership in development of new processes, new substances, and new materials.

3. *Rationale.*

Public support for basic research is justified, in part, on cultural grounds and, in part, on practical grounds. Our culture includes the premise that learning about ourselves and our environment is an ample basis for encouragement of scientific investigations. In addition, we recognize that our increasing ability to meet the common desire for survival, comfort, health, and freedom from toil is rooted in our increasing comprehension of what goes on within and around us.

Within the cultural basis for science, three prime questions stand out: the structure of the Universe, the makeup of matter, and the mechanism of life processes. The third is probably the strongest human preoccupation: the nature and preservation of life. Since all life processes—birth, growth, reproduction, aging mutation, death—are manifestations of chemical change, understanding chemical reactivity can be seen as the foundation for our ultimate understanding of life. Thus chemistry, along with biology, can properly be placed with astronomy and high energy physics as scientific investigations justifiable because they contribute to human knowledge in areas of universal philosophical significance.

However, that does not complete the justification for increasing our understanding of chemical reactivity. It is just as convincingly based upon practical grounds. The development of new processes and new materials depends upon our understanding and control of chemical change. Fundamental advances here will present avenues for innovation that can be exploited in the study of combustion, corrosion and electrochemistry, polymer formation, tailored organic molecules, and new solid state materials. It responds to our need to develop new energy sources, to provide alternate materials for nonrenewable or scarce materials, and to maintain economic competitiveness, all while attentively protecting our environment. It permits the U.S. to produce billions of pounds of organic chemicals, at low cost, in high yield, and with minimum waste product. Combined with our 1981 production of 9.8 billion pounds of synthetic fibers (such as polyesters), 28 billion pounds of plastics (such as polyethylene) and 4.4 billion pounds of synthetic rubber, this capability accounts for the total business volume mentioned earlier, an amount exceeding $175 billion with its current international trade surplus of $12 billion.

This is surely a time of special opportunity to deepen our fundamental knowledge of why and how chemical changes take place. The advance of the frontiers of molecular dynamics has undergone a revolutionary acceleration during the last decade. At the same time, synthetic chemists are exponentially increasing the number of known molecular structures, and constantly adding to our arsenal of reaction types and classes of compounds. Much of this can be attributed to the development and application, during the last two decades, of an array of powerful instrumental and analytical techniques. A few examples show that we have new capabilities in hand with which to probe far beyond current frontiers.

MOLECULAR DYNAMICS

Lasers by themselves have spectacularly expanded our experimental horizons over the last decade. Their short pulse durations permit easy probing of chemical reactions that occur in less than a millionth of a second down to times a thousand-fold shorter (from a microsecond to a nanosecond). With more complex (and more expensive) equipment, chemists are now entering a time domain still another thousand-fold shorter (to a picosecond). Lasers also provide tunable, extremely narrow frequency light sources, implying vastly greater diagnostic sensitivity and selectivity. Finally, lasers give us extremely high light intensities, either in the form of short pulses of ultrahigh power or as continuous light sources with unprecedented photon flux.

Computers also make important contributions to this revolution, both in experimental and theoretical chemistry. They are now common components of experimental

assemblies and a number of the chemist's more sophisticated instruments have built-in (dedicated) computer capability as an essential element. (For example, fourier transform infrared spectrometers, fourier transform nuclear magnetic resonance spectrometers, and X-ray spectrometers). Furthermore, today's computing capability has brought *ab initio* calculations and chemical theory to new levels of fruition.

These are only exemplars—a host of sophisticated instrumental methods ought to be mentioned: molecular beams, ion cyclotron resonance, electron spin resonance, photoelectron spectroscopy, magnetic circular dichroism, resonance Raman, Mossbauer, etc. All of these account for the rich possibilities lying before us. However, the historical basis for funding basic research in chemistry was not premised on the existence (and cost) of such sophisticated equipment. One of the strongest arguments for a large increase in federal support for chemical research is that existing levels do not provide sufficient access to these state-of-the-art techniques and without them, U.S. science will fall behind in areas crucial to our national well-being.

Turning to these new frontiers, the advance of understanding of *molecular dynamics* is one of the most rapidly moving. Here are some of the new phenomena we can now explore.

• *Fast chemical processes in real time.* The primary processes of numerous chemical changes are determined by dynamical events that are intrinsically fast. Many solution phase reactions, photochemical reactions, electron solvation, molecular reorientation in liquids, and reactions of certain biological systems can now be watched "in real time" on the nanosecond-to-picosecond time scale.

• *Energy transfer and movement.* In all chemical changes, the pathways for energy movement are determining factors. Competition among these pathways (including energy dissipation) determines the product yields, the product-state distributions, and the rate at which reaction proceeds. Chemists are now able to track these pathways: radiation, internal conversion, intersystem crossing, intramolecular and intermolecular energy transfer, unimolecular decomposition.

• *Ab initio calculations of reaction surfaces*. With today's computers, the structure and stability of any molecular compound with up to 3 first-row atoms (carbon, nitrogen, oxygen, fluorine) plus various numbers of hydrogen atoms can be calculated almost to the best accuracy available through experiment. This opens to the chemist many situations not readily accessible to experimental measurement. Short-lived reaction intermediates, excited states, and even saddle points of reaction can now be understood, at least for small polyatomic molecules. In a major advance, we can now calculate the forces on all of the atoms during their reorganization from reactant to product molecule geometries.

• *State-to-state chemistry*. Major developments in molecular beam technology, including mass spectrometric ("universal") detectors, vacuum technology, laser excitation, and supersonic jet sources, have enormously broadened their applicability. In the ultimate experiment, reactants can be brought together in precisely known energetic states, with every quantum number fixed, and then the product energies and relative probabilities can be established in the same detail.

• *Mode-selective chemistry*. With high-power, sharply tunable lasers, it is possible to excite one particular degree of freedom for many molecules in a bulk sample. As long as this situation persists, such molecules react as if this degree of freedom is at a very high temperature while all the rest of the molecular degrees of freedom are cold. The chemistry of such selective excitation could potentially reveal the importance and role of that particular degree of freedom in facilitating reaction. To extract this valuable information, energy redistribution and relaxation must be brought under control, and this frontier is being explored.

• *Multiphoton excitation*. One of the most surprising discoveries of the 1970's was that powerful pulsed lasers could highly excite the vibrational degrees of freedom of a molecule on a time scale short compared to molecular collision times. With many tens of quanta of vibrational excitation, the molecule displays unusual chemical pathways. This opens a new type of photochemistry with unique possibilities, the first of which to be recognized was isotope enrichment.

The rich potentialities of these techniques promise to show us how reactions proceed over their entire course. We will at last be able to understand the unstable situations intervening between reactants and products. To realize these benefits, there must be wider access to the sophisticated instrumentation (including computing capability) and the cadre of bright young scientists attracted to this area must be encouraged and increased.

REACTION PATHWAYS

A manifestation of this increasing understanding and control of chemical reactivity is the rapid advance now taking place in devising new reaction pathways in synthetic chemistry. This progress presents a high leverage opportunity since herein lies the foundation of future developments of new products and new processes.

Again powerful instrumental techniques play a central role. The rapid and definitive identification of reaction products, both in composition and structure, accounts for the speed with which synthetic chemists are able to test and develop their synthetic strategies. The nuclear magnetic resonance and mass spectra show what elements are present and the structural environment of virtually every atom. The X-ray crystal structure reveals the complete molecular structure: the interatomic distances, bond angles, and even the right- or left-handedness when mirror-image relationships are present. Spectroscopic techniques, as well, have been essential to progress in the rapidly developing area of organometallic chemistry. The visible and infrared spectra of transition metal complexes reveal electronic configurations and bonding, the foundation for clarifying mechanisms for ligand substitution and electron-transfer processes.

• *Selective pathways in organic synthesis.* Selectivity is the key challenge to the synthetic chemist—to make a precise structural change to a single desired product. The different intrinsic reactivity in each bond type must be recognized (chemoselectivity), reactants must be brought together in proper orientation (regioselectivity) and the desired three-dimensional spatial relations must be obtained (stereoselectivity). The degree to which this type of control can be achieved is shown in the synthesis of the substance adamantane ($C_{10}H_{14}$). This novel molecule resembles in structure a 10-atom "chip" off of a diamond crystal. In a *tour de force*, it was originally produced by a many-step process in only 2.4% yield. Recent research in polycyclic hydrocarbon synthesis now gives adamantane in one step in 75% yield. Then, a surprise practical payoff came when it was discovered that adding a single amine substituent to adamantane gave adamantine (1-amino-adamantane), which proved to be an antiviral agent, a prophylactic drug for influenza, and a drug to combat Parkinson's disease.

The recent development of new ways to construct cyclic five-membered rings has again paid off handsomely. The diverse array of applications includes production of thienamycin, $C_{13}H_{14}N_2SO_4$, a novel relative of penicillin and an important new drug. At another extreme, large ring compounds have been exceptionally difficult to synthesize. Their structures are complicated by functionally crucial left/right-handed structural geometrics ("chiral centers"). Their wide ranging biological properties—from pleasant fragrances for perfumes to anti-fungal, anti-tumor, and antibiotic activities—make large ring synthesis an interesting challenge. An

example is erythromycin, $C_{37}H_{68}O_{12}N$, which in the desired atomic hookup can be shaped into 262,144 different structures derived from the many possible ways to couple the right- and left-handedness at its 18 chiral centers ($2^{18} = 262,144$). Twenty-five years ago, this compound was judged to be "hopelessly complex" by R. B. Woodward, who won the Nobel Prize for synthesizing molecules as complex as quinine and vitamin B_{12}. Today we can aspire to such a goal, in part because of the development of specially designed templates that bring together the terminal atoms of a fourteen-atom chain to form a fourteen-membered ring. This provides the structural framework of erythromycin and it has already resulted in the synthesis of a number of constituents of musk and contributed to our understanding of smell.

• *Crossing inorganic/organic boundaries.* The traditional line of demarkation between organic and inorganic chemists has virtually disappeared as the list of fascinating metal-organic compounds continues to grow. The ubiquitous appearance of these compounds in biological systems underscores the importance of encouraging this cross-boundary research. Furthermore, research in developing new inorganic substances has provided a surprising dividend in their frequent applicability in organic synthesis.

The latter situation is illustrated by the borohydrides. The cohesive picture we have, at last, for this strange boron/hydrogen family was not possible before their study by X-ray crystallography, infrared and NMR spectroscopy, and molecular orbital theory. Now borohydrides are widely used as selective, mild reducing agents in organic synthesis. Silicon and transition-metal organometallic compounds give other examples. Silicon compounds, for example, are used to fold an extended molecular reactant precisely as needed to synthesize the molecule cortisone. Now this valuable therapeutic agent can be made in less than 20 steps at a yield 1000 times higher than achieved in the earlier 50-step process.

Compounds with metal atoms sandwiched between organic rings continue to proliferate and their chemistry will likely relate to catalysis. The metal-organic complexes provide another active synthetic field, with interest both in catalysis and, perhaps, in radioactive or metal-waste cleanup.

• *Novel solids*. Chemists are learning how to prepare solids with quite remarkable properties. Thus, families of solid substances are being synthesized which, like the alumina-silicates (the "zeolites"), are deliberately contrived to include particular shaped cavities and channels. Guest molecules that slip comfortably into these channels can be held in favored conformations as reactants bring about desired chemical changes. The result is that only particular molecules (the ones that fit) react and they do so in a structurally specific way. Entirely different sorts of solids are giving new families of electrically conducting materials. The lead molybdenum sulfide, $PbMo_6S_8$, is a superconductor that can remain superconducting up to 600 kilogauss fields. One of the several conducting organic materials is polyacetylene which, on exposure to various chemicals (iodine, arsenic trifluoride, etc.), can approach metallic conductivities. Polysulfurnitride, $(SN)_x$, not only rivals metal conductivity, it also displays superconductivity. Another promising class of new linear-chain polymer conductors are those based upon metallo-macrocycle complexes held together by bridging groups and treated with an electron-accepting compound. This class is amenable to a wide range of electronically significant chemical modification, hence tailoring to intended application.

Pressure as a controlling dimension of solid state reactions has long been recognized but little understood. With techniques now available, solids can be compressed and studied spectroscopically up to a few hundred thousand atmospheres pressure. New molecular structures, reactivities and electronic properties can be obtained. Photochromic materials provide an example.

Substances like the anils, spiropyranes, and bianthrones change color when exposed to light. Under pressure, the colors can be "tuned" and some of these materials will display the color change merely by heating, without the need for exposure to light. These effects are attributable to changes in molecular structures and electronic makeup which, in turn, can affect chemical reactivity.

Solid state chemistry is relatively less active in the U.S. than abroad; French, German, and Japanese chemists have leadership positions. Hence, there can be a high return if more activity can be stimulated here in the synthesis and characterization of radically new solids. There will emerge new semiconductors, solid state ionic materials (used in batteries, memory devices, display devices, and chemical sensors), ferroelectrics, pyroelectrics, and magnetic materials. Creative synthetic chemists must be attracted and encouraged in this area.

• *Pathways using light as a reagent*. Another promising chemical pathway is connected with the use of light photons in chemical synthesis. Many organic molecules display quite different chemistry and structures after absorption of light. Photosynthesis provides the most striking prototype and our understanding is advancing rapidly. "Artificial photosynthesis" both mimicking Nature and generalizing into new directions is under active study. Chemical storage of solar energy is an obvious long-term goal. In addition, new routes in chemical synthesis are offered. Some high energy ("strained") molecular structures, including those of many natural products, must be formed in energy-consuming (endothermic) processes (e.g., the mycin antibiotics, certain alkaloids, vitamin D precursors, and certain steroid hormones). It is difficult to put in this energy because the active reagents tend to threaten the fragile product. In the photochemically induced process, less aggressive reactants can be used which can be excited with light to approach the product gently from above, with delicate control through the photolysis wavelength. A single example shows the great potential. A calcium homeostatic steroid hormone with the formula $C_{26}H_{44}O_2$ (1,25-dihydrovitamin D_3) can be synthesized photochemically. By using tuned laser light controlled to the optimum wavelength (300nm), the synthetic yield of the desired structure has been increased 400%. How important such light-assisted chemistry will be remains to be seen. Chemists understand the ground state (unexcited) chemistry of literally millions of compounds. Virtually every one of these compounds has different chemistry after light absorption but we have explored only a miniscule fraction of this new domain!

4. *Collaboration*

The thrust toward *understanding chemical reactivity* has inviting avenues for collaboration across traditional disciplinary boundaries. Much of the most fundmental work on molecular dynamics is at the chemistry-physics interface and it specially benefits from close interaction between chemists and physicists on the one hand and between experimentalists and theoreticians on the other. In a similar way, exciting new horizons in synthesis are bringing together the perspectives and techniques of individuals who used to be differentiated as inorganic or organic chemists. Collaborative mechanisms should be encouraged.

B. *Chemical Catalysis*

1. *Program.*

We propose an initiative to apply the techniques of chemistry to obtain a molecular-level understanding of catalysts. Ultimately, new catalyst systems will result that will lay the foundation for the development of new chemical technologies. The program will emphasize research in four areas:

Heterogeneous catalysis: to apply the powerful new instrumental techniques of surface science to the study of chemistry on the surface of a solid.

• *Homogeneous catalysis*: to take advantage of recent developments in synthetic chemistry that show promise as new soluble catalysts.

• *Photocatalysis and electrocatalysis*: to investigate the rich possibilities of solution chemistry catalytically assisted by electrode processes, with and without absorption of light.

• *Artificial-enzyme catalysis*: to bring together chemists' ability to synthesize molecules of predesigned topography and the biochemists' emerging understandings of natural catalysts, the enzymes. We should be able to generate a new class of artificial enzyme-like catalysts tailored to specific needs.

2. *Objectives.*

• To identify the fundamental molecular ingredients of catalytic processes in order, ultimately, to guide the development of chemical high technology.

• To synthesize new catalysts that may serve as the foundation of new chemical processes.

• To increase the number of young scientists who have the breadth and background needed to contribute to the field of chemical catalysis.

• To provide the fundamental knowledge and creative manpower required for the U.S. to maintain competitive advantage in catalysis-aided technologies.

3. *Rationale.*

A catalyst accelerates chemical reactions toward equilibrium without being consumed. This acceleration can be as much as ten orders of magnitude. A *selective* catalyst can have this same dramatic effect but on only one of many competing reactions. While the development of new catalysts was empirical fifteen years ago, research innovations in chemical sciences over the last ten years are converting catalysis from art to science. A familiar example displays the benefits to be gained—the catalytic converter developed for automobiles to reduce air pollution. The catalyst—containing two grams of platinum, palladium, and rhodium per car—oxidizes unburned hydrocarbons and carbon monoxide to harmless water and carbon dioxide. Simultaneously, it reduces toxic nitrogen oxides to harmless nitrogen gas.

Estimates that twenty percent of the gross national product is generated through the use of catalysis demonstrate the major role industrial catalysis has in satisfying such diverse societal needs as food production, energy conversion, defense technologies, environmental protection and health care. On the horizon is the extensive use of catalysts to tap new energy sources—such as heavy oils, coal, oil shale, tar sands, lignites, and biomass—as we run out of oil. However, American preeminence in catalysis science is now challenged by Japan, Germany, the USSR, and France. These countries have established institutional networks to accelerate research and development in this evolving high-technology field. To meet this challenge, we must keep our own catalytic science vital.

Industrial research in catalysis is critically dependent on the techniques and concepts which have been developed in university and National Laboratories. Since industrial laboratories use the latest surface science and laser spectroscopic techniques, they want their new young scientists to bring with them state-of-the-art experience. Furthermore, industrial catalysis research must be chosen with an eye toward existing technology and product lines. Industry cannot sustain the adventurous fundamental research that will underlie the discovery of radically new catalysts. To illustrate this, consider the enormously important conversion of atmospheric nitrogen into ammonia. The original work by Haber in Germany produced an ammonia yield of 13% per pass. Today the same process is used on a massive scale. Yet, seventy years after Haber's work, a modern ammonia unit producing some 1500 tons per day operates at only slightly greater yield per pass

(perhaps 15%). There is no physical limitation here—equilibrium is on our side. What is needed is fundamental research in catalysis. This is a role for university chemists. It is a place for federal investment.

This chemical catalysis program will concentrate on long-term research to learn about catalytic processes on the molecular level. Then the new fundamental knowledge generated will be transferred into technology by the employment of the emerging young scientists in industry and by the ties formed in this program among scientists in the universities, the National Laboratories and industry.

HETEROGENEOUS CATALYSIS

Heterogeneous catalysts are solid materials prepared with large surface areas (1-500 m^2/g) upon which chemical reactions occur at extremely high rate and selectivity. Some major new commercial processes based on heterogeneous catalyst developments in recent years include:

— "reforming" hydrocarbons to high octane composition (platinum alloy catalysts);
— "cracking" high paraffins to gasoline (molecular sieve catalysts);
— methanol to gasoline, jet fuel (molecular sieve catalysts);
— exhaust converter on automobiles (platinum, palladium, rhodium catalysts);
— ethylene oxidation to ethylene oxide (silver, cesium, chlorine catalyst);
— propylene oxidation to acrolein and acrylonitrile (bismuth, and molybdenum oxide catalyst);
— ethylene polymerization (chromium catalyst);
— propylene polymerization (titanium, magnesium oxide catalyst).

Surface science is developing rapidly and now gives us experimental access to this two-dimensional reaction domain. Because of the unsatisfied bonding capability of the atoms at the surface, chemistry here is dramatically different from that of the same reactants brought together in solution or the gas phase. But when chemists are able to "see" what molecular structures are on the surface, then all of our knowledge of reactions in conventional settings becomes applicable. This will open the door to understanding and controlling the chemistry in this surface domain. There are five areas of heterogeneous catalysis where this understanding will have major impact on new chemical technologies.

• *Molecular sieve synthesis and catalysis.* Molecular sieves are crystalline alumina-silicates containing pores or channels within which chemical reactions can be initiated. They offer unparalleled efficiency both for cracking of petroleum and for conversions such as shale oil or methanol to gasoline. We need to know better how to synthesize molecular sieves with controlled molecular pore size, as well as to determine the elementary reaction steps and intermediates that account for their efficacy.

• *Metal catalysis.* Finely dispersed transition metals are already coming into use to catalyze hydrocarbon conversions and ammonia synthesis for fertilizers. Other such applications and improved performance will follow from intensive research into the control of surface structures, oxidation states, residence time of reaction intermediates, and resistance to catalyst "poisons" (such as sulfur).

• *Substitutes for precious metal catalysts.* Many of the most effective catalysts are rare metals not available in the U.S., including rhodium, platinum, palladium, and ruthenium. Their strategic value requires a concerted research effort to find more accessible substitutes, such as transition metal oxides, carbides, sulfides, and nitrides.

• *Conversion catalysts.* We must find catalysts to convert abundant substances to useful fuels and industrial feedstocks. These reactions include conversion of atmospheric

nitrogen to nitrates, methane to methanol, carbon dioxide to formate, and depolymerization of coal and biomass to useful hydrocarbons.

• *Catalysts to improve air and water quality.* We have many environmental pollution problems for which we need to match the spectacular success of the catalytic converter used to clean automobile exhaust gases. To begin, we need catalysts that remove sulfur oxides from smoke plumes, that purify water, and that prevent acid rain.

As we learn more about the molecular structures at the solid-gas interface (reactants, intermediates and products), a better understanding of surface chemical bonding will follow. We can look forward to understanding additives that modify catalyst performance ("promoters" and "poisons"). Then, the challenging subject of synthesis of the designed catalyst can be addressed. All of this fundamental knowledge will underlie and facilitate the development of new and more selective heterogeneous catalysts.

HOMOGENEOUS CATALYSIS

Homogeneous catalysts are soluble and active in a liquid reaction medium. Often they are complex metal-containing molecules whose structures can be modified to tune reactivity in desired directions to achieve very high selectivities. (In this sense homogeneous catalysts can be superior to heterogeneous ones.) The largest industrial-scale process using homogeneous catalysis is the partial oxidation of para-xylene to terephthalic acid (United States production in 1981 was 6.2 billion pounds per year), which uses dissolved salts of cobalt and manganese as the catalyst system. Most of the product ends up polymerized to give us polyester clothing, tire cord, soft drink bottles, and a host of other useful articles.

An important branch of homogeneous catalysis has developed from research in organometallic chemistry. An example is rhodium dicarbonyl diiodide, employed in the commercial production of acetic acid from methanol and carbon monoxide. With this catalyst present, the reaction economically gives more than 99% selectivity to acetic acid.

There are three areas of homogeneous catalysis with potential for major impact on new chemical technologies from increased understanding.

- *Activation of inert molecules.* There are a number of relatively inert molecules that are enticing as reaction feedstocks because of their abundance: nitrogen, carbon monoxide, carbon dioxide, and methane. One way to approach this end might be through homogeneous organometallic catalysis. Dramatic examples of this promise are beginning to appear. Soluble compounds of tungsten and molybdenum with molecular nitrogen have been prepared and induced to produce ammonia under mild conditions. The carbon-hydrogen bonds in normally unreactive hydrocarbons have been split by organorhodium and organoiridium complexes. Hope for build-up of complex molecules from one-carbon molecules, such as carbon monoxide, is encouraged by recent demonstrations of carbon-carbon bond formation at metal centers bound in soluble metal-organic molecules. Synthesis of compounds with multiple bonds between carbon and metal atoms has had a major impact in clarifying the catalytic interconversion of olefins. While there is much to learn, the stakes are high and the odds for success are excellent.

- *Metal cluster chemistry.* An adventurous frontier of catalysis lies in the expanding capability of chemists to synthesize molecules built around several metal atoms in proximity (a "metal cluster"). In parallel, solution and cryogenic techniques are revealing the structures and chemistry of small aggregates containing only metal ions or atoms ("naked clusters"). All of these clusters, bound or "naked", furnish a natural

bridge between homogeneous catalysis and bulk metal, heterogeneous catalysis.

Many directions are being explored. Cubical units of four metal atoms and four sulfur atoms are now known for iron, nickel, tungsten, zinc, cobalt, manganese, and chromium. This "cubane" structure for iron has been found to be the functional unit in the ferrodoxin iron proteins that catalyze electron transfer reactions in biological systems. Many cluster compounds have been made from metals bound to carbon monoxide. These metal carbonyls have formulas $M_x(CO)_y$, and x can be made very large. (The world's record as of this writing is a platinum compound with $x = 38$.) It is intriguing that many of the most catalytically active metals also form cluster compounds (e.g., rhodium, platinum, osmium, ruthenium, iridium, etc.). Now the chemistry of these elements can be studied as a function of cluster size.

- *Stereoselective catalysts.* Another exciting frontier involves the development of homogeneous stereoselective catalysts. Many biological molecules can have either of two geometric structures connected by mirror-image (chiral) relationships, and generally only one of these structures is functionally useful in the biological system. If a complex molecule has seven such chiral carbon atoms and a synthetic process produces all of the mirror-image structures in equal amounts, there would be $2^7 = 128$ structures, 127 of which might have no activity or, worse, some undesired effect. Thus the ability to synthesize preferentially the desired structure with the desired geometry at every chiral center is essential.

Immense strides in this area are being made. For example, L-dopa, an amino acid that has revolutionized the treatment of Parkinson's disease, is now made using an asymmetric addition of hydrogen to a carbon-carbon double bond. The catalyst is a soluble rhodium phosphine catalyst that gives 96% of the correct structure with high efficiency. Stereospecific oxidations can also be carried out. The recent invention of a titanium catalyst to add, in a specific geometry, an oxygen atom across a carbon-carbon double bond has lowered the price of gypsy moth attractant ten-fold. Despite these successes, the basic factors that produce stereochemical control are not at all well understood. Mechanistic studies are needed and the rewards from better understanding will be great.

Future advances in homogeneous catalysis are dependent upon easy access to advanced instrumental techniques: X-rays, high-field nuclear magnetic resonance, electron spin resonance, mass spectroscopy, and computational facilities. Further, work at the interfaces between organic, inorganic and physical chemistry is involved, so breadth of knowledge is especially important.

Photocatalysis and Electrocatalysis

Exciting advances have recently been made in the study and control of chemistry taking place at the interface between a liquid solution and an electrochemical electrode surface. In some applications, the chemistry is initiated by absorption of light by a semiconductor used as an electrode. Whether light is involved (photocatalysis) or not (electrocatalysis), this rapidly moving field depends upon our knowledge both of homogeneous catalysis and of semiconductor behavior.

- *Photoelectrochemical cells.* There is considerable promise from research directed toward conversion of light to electrical energy in a photoelectrochemical cell. In such a cell, one or both of the electrodes is a semiconductor material that absorbs the incident light. The lure is that semiconductors, probably with chemically modified surfaces, can absorb red and infrared light, the spectral region within which most solar energy falls.

Chemists are learning how to bond dyes and protective polymers to the surface of a semiconductor solid through covalent bonds.

There is now the potential for solving the key problems of photoelectrochemical cells: to catalyze the essential electron-transfer reactions with solution species, to prevent chemical erosion of the electrode, to avoid back-reaction, and to shape the active spectral region to match that of the energy source, the sun. Already cells for conversion of solar energy to electrical energy have rivaled those of solid state photovoltaic cells (e.g., the n-GaAs/selenide system operates at 14% efficiency). Numerous ''non-conventional'' semiconductors are under investigation, such as TiO_2, CdS, WSe_2. These materials are still speciality products but there is good prospect that they will cost much less than existing single crystal photovoltaic materials.

- *Photocatalysis.* Related studies involving photoelectrochemical cells or suspensions of semiconductor materials focus attention on the chemistry that can be brought about. In these systems, light absorbed in the semiconductor promotes catalytic oxidation-reduction chemistry at the electrode-solution or at a membrane-solution interface. Such oxidation-reduction chemistry has significant scientific interest and, likely, great practical significance. For example, photo-destruction of a toxic waste material such as cyanide has been demonstrated at titanium dioxide surfaces. A more popularized and perhaps feasible concept is that such photo-catalytic chemistry, solar energy driven, could produce massive amounts of hydrogen and oxygen from the photoelectrolysis of water. What an intriguing prospect, to convert from diminishing and seriously polluting petroleum fuels to a renewable fuel that burns to water and that is made from water using energy from the sun.

- *Electrocatalysis.* Apart from light-initiated processes, electrode surfaces with catalytic activity offer a new domain for chemical synthesis. In a field with a long heritage, recent developments have shown that electrode surfaces can be chemically tailored to promote particular reactions. This research area has adopted techniques from the semiconductor industry (such as chemical vapor deposition) and coupled them with imaginative synthetic chemical techniques for surface modification.

An example is the electrocatalyst family developed for use in chlorine generation in chlor-alkali cells. A successful case is based upon a thin layer of ruthenium dioxide (the catalyst) deposited on a base metal electrode. This electrocatalyst has dramatically changed practice in the chlor-alkali industry (an industry representing billions of dollars in sales) because of its improved energy efficiency and reduced cell maintenance. Future developments will include radically improved fuel cells, which provide clean and thermodynamically efficient conversion of chemical fuels to electricity.

• *Chemistry at the solid/liquid interface.* Before the technological potentialities of any of the above can be realized, we must have a much better understanding of the nature of chemistry at the semiconductor/liquid interface. The marvelous instrumentation developed for surface science studies is, of course, applicable only at solid/vacuum interfaces. We need comparable capability at the solid/liquid boundary. This capability will be won from fundamental research in solid state chemistry, electrochemistry, surface analysis, and surface spectroscopy. Where the biggest gains are to be made is a speculative question. The surprising discovery of the million-fold intensification involved in surface-enhanced Raman effect encourages optimism.

The potential gains from these exciting areas are considerable. We need to know how to catalyze multielectron transfer reactions at an electrode surface. That is the chemistry required, for example, to photogenerate a liquid fuel such as methanol from carbon dioxide and water. Multielectron transfer catalytic electrodes for oxygen reduction in electrochemical cells would find a welcoming home in the fuel cell industry.

It is also likely that research on semiconductor electrode surface modification will reflect back beneficially into the field of electronics. Thus, the integrated circuit technology based upon GaAs may depend upon control of its surface chemistry. Already photoresist/chemical etching techniques are recognizing the importance of the chemistry involved in surface modification (witness the pursuit of "anisotropic chemical etching").

In summary, our evolving understanding of the electrode/solution interface, buttressed by concepts based on semiconductor electrodes and the development of a number of new methods for modifying electrode surfaces, has provided powerful new approaches to both photocatalysis and electrocatalysis. Future advances will benefit synergistically from progress in heterogeneous and homogeneous catalysis, increased understanding of mass and charge transport within the electrode surface layers, and continued development of experimental methods and theoretical models for the interface.

ARTIFICIAL-ENZYME CATALYSIS

The most striking benefit from our bounteous knowledge of reaction pathways and the analytical capacity of modern instrumentation has been the development of capability to deal with molecular systems of extreme complexity. With the synthetic chemist's prowess and such diagnostic instruments as nuclear magnetic resonance, X-ray spectroscopy, and mass spectroscopy we can now synthesize and control the structure of molecules that approach biological complexity. This includes the ability to fix the molecular shape, even extending to the mirror-image properties that are so crucial to biological function.

There is no application of these capabilities more intriguing than coupling them with our growing knowledge of catalysis to synthesize artificial enzymes. In Nature, enzymes are the biological catalysts that accelerate a wide variety of chemical reactions at the modest temperatures at which living organisms can survive. A given enzyme selects from a many-component system a single reactant molecule and transforms it to a single product with prescribed chiral geometry.

Without catalysts, many simple reactions are extremely slow under ambient conditions. Raising the temperature speeds things up, but this may include a variety of undesired outcomes—acceleration of unwanted reactions, destruction of delicate products, and waste of energy. Hence, there are strong reasons to develop synthetic catalysts that work like enzymes. First, natural enzymes do not exist for most of the chemical reactions in which we have interest. In the manufacture of polymers, synthetic fibers, medicinal compounds, and many industrial chemicals, very few of the reactions used could be catalyzed by naturally occurring enzymes. Even where there are natural enzymes, their properties are not ideal for chemical manufacture. Enzymes are proteins, sensitive substances that are easily denatured and destroyed. In those industries that do use enzymes, major effort is directed toward modifying them to make them more stable.

• *Controlled molecular topography and designed catalysts.* We have a pretty good idea how enzymes work. Nature contrives a molecular surface fitted to a specific reactant. This surface attracts from a mixture the unique molecular type desired and immobilizes it. Held on the surface, the selected reactant is forced to abandon its flexibility and assume a distinct shape. When the reaction partner arrives, the scene is set for the desired reaction to take place in the desired geometry.

Organic chemists who have taken up this challenge are making excellent progress. Without special control, large molecules usually have exclusively convex surfaces (ball-like shapes). So a first step has been to learn to synthesize large molecules with concave surfaces. Then, these concave surfaces could be shaped to accommodate a desired reactant. Cyclodextrins provide examples—they are toroidal in shape. The crown ethers, developed over the last 15 years, have a quite dif-

ferent surface topography. For instance, 18-crown-6 consists of twelve carbon atoms and six oxygen atoms evenly spaced in a cyclic arrangement. In the presence of potassium ions, the ether takes up a crown-like structure in which the six oxygen atoms point toward and bind a potassium ion. Lithium and sodium ions are too small and rubidium ions too large to fit in the crown-shaped cavity, so this ether preferentially extracts potassium ions from a mixture. Much more ornate examples now exist. Chiral binaphthyl units can be coupled into cylindrical or egg-shaped cavities. With benzene rings, enforced cavities have been made with the shapes of bowls, pots, saucers, and vases.

Plainly we are moving toward the next step, to build into these shaped cavities a catalytic binding site. The earliest successes will likely be patterned after natural enzymes but there is no doubt that in time, artificial, enzyme-like catalysts will not be limited by what we can find already known in Nature.

• *Biomimetic enzymes.* A short-cut approach is to pattern artificial enzymes closely after natural enzymes. This has been called "biomimetic chemistry." As examples, mimics have been prepared for the enzymes that biologically synthesize amino acids. The artificial enzymes incorporate the important catalytic groups of a natural enzyme (vitamin B_6, for example) and show good selectivity, even including the formation of the correct chirality in the product. Mimics have been prepared for several of the common enzymes involved in the digestion of proteins, e.g., substances that catalyze the cleavage of RNA have been synthesized based upon the catalytic groups found in the enzyme ribonuclease. Mimics have also been synthesized which imitate the class of enzymes called cytochromes P-450, which are involved in many biological oxidations, and the oxygen carrier hemoglobin. Furthermore, mimics have been prepared for biological membranes and for those molecules which carry substances through membranes. These have potential applications in the construction of organized systems to perform selective absorption and detection, as in living cells.

It is important for the U.S. to build on its early lead in this field. Although most of the work mentioned above has been done in the U.S., the Japanese have also become extremely active and have specifically targeted "biomimetic chemistry" as an area of special opportunity. Research on synthetic organic chemistry develops novel methods to construct the required molecule, and elaborates new kinds of structures. The study of detailed reaction mechanisms in organic and biological chemistry permits a rational approach to catalyst design. This is an area ripe for development, deserving special encouragement as a part of this program in Chemical Catalysis.

4. *Collaboration.*

Thus, catalysis research with the four facets named here involves many subfields of chemistry (surface chemistry, solid state chemistry, organic synthesis, inorganic synthesis, photochemistry, electrochemistry, bioorganic chemistry and chemical engineering) along with the contiguous fields of solid state physics, surface physics, biology, and biochemistry. Each of these different perspectives is needed to address fully the common goal, to understand how a catalyst intermediary can enhance preferentially the rate at which a desired reaction takes place. Hence, there is great opportunity for collaboration across disciplinary boundaries.

C. *Chemistry of Life Processes*

1. *Program.*

We propose an initiative to develop and apply the techniques of chemistry and the skills of individuals knowledgeable in that discipline to the solution of molecular-level problems in life processes. This initiative includes both the application of chemical science to biology, and the development of new chemical science based on stimuli provided by biology. Research at this border between chemistry and biology requires individuals broadly competent in both areas, and a special effort must be made to develop such individuals.

The program will emphasize the molecular aspects of six areas.

• Enzymology: to understand the molecular interactions responsible for natural enzymatic activity and its inhibition; to produce natural enzymes for use in chemical synthesis.
• Immunochemistry: to learn the chemical basis of the immune and allergenic response; use, function, and modification of monoclonal antibodies; synthesis of antigens and adjuvants.
• Chemical Endocrinology: to synthesize hormones and hormone analogs; to understand hormone agonist and antagonist mechanisms.
• Neurochemistry: to determine the molecular basis of nerve transmission, neurotransmitters, agonist and antagonist chemistry, and membrane polarization.
• Membrane Chemistry and Vectorial Chemistry: to clarify active and passive transport (bioenergetics).
• Biological Model Studies: to understand host/guest chemistry, semisynthetic enzymes, and active sites.

2. *Objectives.*

• To strengthen basic research in the life sciences by providing the molecular-scale analytical, synthetic, and structural techniques required to identify, prepare, and study the organic chemical compounds which are central to modern molecular biology.
• To accelerate the conversion of qualitative biological information into techniques and substances useful in human and animal medicine and agriculture.
• To educate graduate students and postdoctoral fellows in both chemistry and biology; to provide individuals skilled in chemistry (especially organic synthesis, organic reaction mechanisms, and analytical

chemistry), who can understand and interpret biological problems and opportunities in molecular terms.

3. *Rationale*.

The study of the molecular bases of the reactions occurring in life offers enormous opportunity both for discovery in basic physical science and for application to human health, animal health, and agriculture. This area of research includes some of the most important problems which now exist in science. Solutions to these problems will have very large and beneficial impacts on society.

Biology has evolved a range of problems of revolutionary significance that now require analysis in terms of molecular interactions. The molecular synthesis and analysis required for the solutions of these problems can only be provided by chemistry.

A major fraction of biology can be reduced to two broad types of problems at the molecular level:

Receptor-Substrate Interactions

Essentially all biological processes are mediated by the selective interaction of a protein receptor (enzyme, antibody, membrane and intracellular receptors) with one or more specific substrates (enzyme substrate, antigen, hormone, neurotransmitter, or simple molecule or ion).

To study these processes in molecular detail, and to control them with the precision required for rational applications in medicine, agriculture, and other areas, it is necessary to be able to:

• isolate and identify the structures of endogenous substrates or substrate analogs;
• synthesize these substrates and analogs in useful quantities and high purity;
• analyze their interactions with their receptors both in physical-chemical and biological terms;
• modify their structures to give useful

agonist and antagonist activity and to facilitate effective delivery into living organisms.

The development of analytical, structural, synthetic, and mechanistic techniques appropriate to this area of molecular science represents an enormous challenge and opportunity for chemistry. The active substances may be present *in vivo* only in minute quantities; they are usually water soluble (polypeptides, polysaccharides) or surface active (lipids, membrane or hydrophobic proteins); they may have high molecular weights and complex or heterogeneous structures. Medicine and biology need the methods of chemistry to manipulate these substances; chemistry cannot presently provide fully adequate methods. Hence, the challenge and the opportunity for chemists.

Membranes and Vectorial Chemistry

The set of chemical reactions that constitute life take place in cells and organelles. The concept of vectorial chemistry (reactions depending upon spatial separation of reactants into regions of different concentrations—that is, on concentration gradients—for their driving force) is poorly understood at a molecular level, but essential to biochemistry (the Mitchell chemiosmotic hypothesis is the best-known example).

Understanding the relations between concentration gradients across membranes and processes which form or break chemical bonds is a formidable task, one which requires active chemical modeling at both the synthetic and the kinetic level to complement the current activity in mechanistic biology. The related problem of the transport of molecules across membranes (for example, between blood and a particular type of cell) is central to the area of pharmacokinetics and drug delivery.

What reason is there to expect chemistry to be able to make progress on the many specific problems contained in these two major general classes of problems? A number of recent advances in science and engineering have provided an extraordinarily powerful set of techniques which are appropriate for the investigation of problems in chemical biology at the molecular and supramolecular level. Examples are given below.

- Recombinant DNA technology provides the opportunity to prepare proteins in substantial quantities with controlled variations in amino acid sequence.
- Monoclonal antibodies produced in large quantities using hybridoma techniques provide specific receptors against virtually any high or medium molecular weight substance.
- X-ray single crystal analysis can now solve very complex structural problems.
- Electron microscopy permits direct visualization of many structures at levels between 2 and 1000 A and is superbly suited to solving problems in membrane chemistry and in the structures of large molecules.
- Ultrasensitive analytical techniques (fast-atom-bombardment mass spectrometry, two-dimensional NMR spectroscopy, antibody-based competitive binding assays, electron capture gas-liquid chromatography, high performance liquid chromatography) can elucidate structures of small quantities of very complex substances.
- Sophisticated synthetic technology, based both on conventional chemical techniques and on a range of biological techniques, including enzymatic transformation and fermentation, make it possible to synthesize complex naturally occurring substances and analogs in useful quantities.
- Computers permit analysis of the details of receptor-substrate binding, and modeling of the complex set of coupled reactions which take place in living cells.

In summary, molecular biology has become sufficiently detailed that many of its most important current questions must be phrased and answered using chemical methods. Hence, chemical techniques are essential to understanding biological phenomena and for converting this understanding into a form useful in medicine and agriculture. There is a pressing practical reason for accelerating this application of chemistry to biological problems, namely, the economic and technological relevance of chemical biology to biotechnology and applied biology, and the intense international competition in this area. Failure to encourage the chemical aspect of biology will cost us leadership in this area and we will forfeit ownership of the practical results to other countries.

4. *Collaboration.*

An important aspect of the proposed program would be its emphasis on interdisciplinary research. Where appropriate, the program would actively encourage development of collaborative projects which integrate programs of chemical and biological research.

In addition, biotechnology is an area of extremely active industrial research. This derives from the special potential for health care (with efforts by essentially all pharmaceutical companies and by a host of small start-up biotechnology companies) and improvements in agriculture (Monsanto, du Pont, and many others). The major immediate markets being addressed by these companies are high-value proteins (interferon, plasma thrombinogen activator, insulin, serum Factor VIII, animal and human growth hormones, vaccines) and monoclonal antibody products (clinical diagnostics). Longer-term industrial projects are aimed at a range of more complex health-care products (treatments for cancer, diabetes, high blood pressure; methods for organ transplantation; immuno-regulators), improved plant strains, enzymatic catalysts for industrial and food use, biomass utilization for energy, and human genetic engineering.

The ultimate success of this industrial endeavor will depend heavily upon the supply of young scientists with the needed cross-disciplinary expertise. This program will provide such experience through research more basic than but clearly complementary to the major threads of current industrial research. For example, the development of molecular understandings of the reactions in nerve transmission and of oxidative phosphorylation are central to advances in the relevant biology but still far from application. Ultimately, these areas will be central to the development of neuroactive drugs and more efficient plants. Similarly, the development of new synthetic methods for biologically relevant molecules remains primarily an academic activity, but it is critical to the continued leadership of our pharmaceutical industry.

In fact, the scope for new research in chemical biology is so great that full and cooperative effort from both university and industry is both warranted and required. Industry is now actively building on the basic science of recent years (as well as conducting some of its own very excellent basic work); the university must provide the basic science for the next cycle of industrial discovery and development.

III. CONCLUSIONS

Chemistry extends all the way from physics, with its strong ethos of deductive logic, to the largely phenomenological biological sciences. We are at a gratifying period when chemistry is ''hot at both ends.'' With adequate access to the powerful techniques now developing, chemistry can expect to explore and understand the principles that govern chemical change at a much more fundamental level than has been possible in the past. At this end of the spectrum, chemistry can begin to escape the bounds of empiricism imposed thus far by the intractability of many-body theory and the limits of our measurements. Yet, despite these barriers, chemists have been

so enormously successful with their inductive approach that molecules of exquisite complexity can be recognized and synthesized in every intricate detail. This capability is most timely, because the phenomenological advances of the biosciences now demand explication at the molecular level. Thus, the time is ripe for quite spectacular advances in chemistry.

Hence, in the next ten to twenty years, there will be dramatic changes in our basic understandings of chemical change and our ability to marshal those understandings to deliberate purpose. The program presented here is intended to define a leadership role for the U.S., as these advances are won. The rewards accompanying such leadership are commensurate with the prominent role of chemistry in addressing societal needs, in ameliorating the problems of our technological age, and in sustaining our economic well-being. The costs of falling behind are simply intolerable.

To exploit the intellectual opportunities in chemistry and to maximize the social gain, a substantial incremental increase in federal support for basic research in the chemical sciences is needed. This need for enhanced federal investment in chemical research is rooted in a pattern of funding historically appropriate to a test-tube and bunsen burner era, an era long since eclipsed. The sophistication of a modern chemistry laboratory requires a much more vigorous and sustained financial commitment, both in capital investment and in supporting services. The cost is miniscule compared to the stakes involved; we must nurture a $175 billion industry that maintains a $12 billion positive balance of trade and employs over a million people. We must continue to provide it with a full reservoir of fundamental knowledge.

Appendix I

Fundamental Questions Before Us

A. UNDERSTANDING CHEMICAL REACTIVITY

Molecular Dynamics.

a. How is energy redistributed as a function of time if it is deposited in a molecule in a specific excitation?

b. How does the energy in a molecule (amount, states, intramolecular distribution) determine its reactivity?

c. Can the chemistry of a molecule be affected by an intense (but not absorbed) photon field?

d. Can we understand and theoretically predict the detailed energy distribution among the products in bimolecular reactions?

e. Can we observe the transition state in real time?

f. Is there a Franck-Condon aspect to H or H + transfer?

g. How can a non-thermalized distribution of excited states be maintained and can novel chemistry be achieved thereby?

h. Can we fully characterize and understand intramolecular and intermolecular energy transfer processes?

i. Can we store solar energy using artificial photosynthesis?

j. What new reaction mechanisms operate at high temperatures because of unusual gaseous molecules and unusually rapid mobility?

k. Can we understand and predict the unusual chemical species and solid phases formed at high temperatures?

Chemical Pathways.

a. What are the systematics of the metal-ligand bond energies in organometallic compounds?

b. What are the mechanisms and rates of multi-electron transfer reactions and how can they be controlled?

c. Can interfacial energy be used to synthesize new solids with unique structural features (e.g., channels, cavities, holes)?

d. How can metastable non-stoichiometric solids be prepared?

e. How can the dimensionality of a solid be controlled (linear chains, two dimensional nets, sandwich solids, etc.)?

f. What principles govern conformer-selective chemistry?

g. Can synthetic polymers that are dynamic entities be designed?

h. Can novel inorganic solids be made with molecular beam epitaxy?

i. Do topological principles underlie some aspects of chemical structures and reactions?

j. What molecular properties exhibit bistability suitable for digital information storage in a molecular electronics system?

k. Can organic ferromagnetic compounds be synthesized?

l. What are the structural requirements for nonlinear optical properties in organic molecules?

B. CHEMICAL CATALYSIS

Heterogeneous Catalysis.

a. For chemisorbed intermediate species, what are the residence times? Can they be changed to raise catalyst efficiency?

b. For chemisorbed intermediate species, what molecular structures and oxidation states give optimum selectivity?

c. Why are transition metals the best catalysts?

d. What general mechanisms determine catalyst deactivation? Specifically, how do nickel and vanadium compounds deactivate catalysts?

e. What is the combustion process of carbon on catalytic surfaces?

f. What determines surface migration of chemisorbed species on a surface? What role does this migration play in catalysis?

g. Can we identify and characterize active sites in heterogeneous catalysts?

Homogeneous Catalysis.

a. How is the rupture of H-H, C-H, and C-C bonds altered as the size of a metal cluster catalyst increases?

b. What relationships connect homogeneous, metal cluster, and metal surface catalysis?

c. Can we design homogeneous catalysts that would selectively convert coal to specific desired products?

d. How can chiral metal complexes be designed to induce chirality in organic reaction products?

e. Can we achieve selective homogeneous oxidation catalysis for terminal positions in alkanes?

f. Can catalytic Diels-Alder chemistry be developed?

g. Can oxidative fixation of nitrogen (e.g., to nitric acid) be catalyzed?

h. Can the addition of water or ammonia to olefins (to give alcohols and amines) be catalyzed?

Photocatalysis and Electrocatalysis.

a. How does catalysis at the solid-gas interface connect to electrocatalysis at the solid-liquid interfaces?

b. Can we define, control, and understand the electronic structure of surfaces?

c. What principles are involved in the design and synthesis of new electrocatalysts?

d. What principles are involved in the design and synthesis of new semiconductors materials for photoassisted reactions?

e. Can we develop analytical methods to study chemistry at the solid/liquid interface to match the power of those recently developed for use at the solid/vacuum interface?

f. How can light-absorbing dyes be chemically bound to semiconductor surfaces?

Artificial-Enzyme Catalysis.

a. What obstacles impede synthesis of artificial-enzyme catalysts tailored for a desired reaction?

b. Can we design catalysts to fix the structure (head-to-tail, head-to-head, block, etc.) and stereochemistry of polymers?

c. Can we enhance selectivity through surface shape?

d. Can artificial enzymes be designed to operate in organic solvents?

e. Can artificial enzymes be incorporated into artificial membranes to achieve energy-driven transport (as occurs in living cells)?

f. By adding binding sites for regulator molecules, can we design artificial enzymes to act as detectors? Can these be developed with feedback loops to adapt and control their environment?

C. CHEMISTRY OF LIFE PROCESSES

Enzymology.

a. What is the relation between receptor protein/enzyme binding/active site structure and specificity/catalytic activity?

b. What strategies are required to design substrates which compete with endogeneous substrate for specific receptor/active sites?

c. Can enzymes be used as practical catalysts in organic synthesis?

d. What are the mechanisms of enzymatic reactions (e.g., in protein and nucleic acid synthesis, oxidative phosphorylation, photosynthesis, active transport, intermediary metabolism)?

e. Can combined chemical/biological synthetic techniques be developed to improve markedly the synthesis of nucleic acid sequences?

f. What is the atomic-level basis for enzyme tertiary structure and stability?

Immunology.

a. What is the relation between immunoglobin structure and binding specificity?

b. What are the best techniques for producing and purifying monoclonal antibodies?

c. What antigens and adjuvants are most effective in initiating an immune response?

d. How large a fragment of a protein antigen is required to evoke an effective immune response?

e. Can monoclonal antibodies serve as a basis for chemical purification procedures? As starting materials for semisynthetic enzyme production? For new types of chemical analytical schemes?

Endocrinology.

a. What are the structures of important endogenous hormones?

b. What is the best strategy for inferring the binding specificity of hormone receptors?

c. How should one design synthetic hormone analogs that have desired activity, specificity, and *in vivo* lifetime?

d. What synthetic strategies are required to synthesize synthetic hormones and analogs (especially polypeptide hormones)?

Neurochemistry.

a. What are the structures of important neurotransmitters?

b. What related structures will have agonist/antagonist activity?

Membrane Chemistry and Vectorial Chemistry.

a. Is the chemiosmotic hypothesis correct? What is the molecular basis for interconversion of energy stored in concentration gradients and energy stored in reactive chemical bonds?

b. How is charge separation across membranes accomplished in photosynthesis, respiration, and related areas of bioenergetics?

c. What is the molecular basis for active transport processes? Can understanding of these processes be used to suggest new types of abiological membranes having useful selectivity?

d. What is the chemistry of perception (vision, smell, memory)?

e. What is the relation between chemical, physical, and biological properties of lipid membranes? Can synthetic membrane systems (liposomes, others) be developed for drug delivery?

Chemical Studies Relevant to Biological Systems.

a. Can we understand the hydrophobic effect in aqueous solutions?

b. What are the best strategies for the synthesis of water-soluble molecules having biological activity (oligosaccharides, lipids, polypeptides, neuroactive substances, nucleic acids, metabolites)?

c. What are the structural and thermodynamic bases for molecular recognition (host/guest chemistry)?

d. What are the properties of thin hydrocarbon membranes (selectivity, permeability, concentration polarization, interfacial structure, thermodynamics of membrane diffusion)?

e. How are cooperative chemical phenomena related to biological systems (liquid crystals, organized lipid assemblies, oscillating reactions, nucleation and phase transitions)?

f. Can one construct instructive chemical models for important biological phenomena (active transport, photosynthesis, oxidation phosphorylation, proton translocation, muscular contraction, information storage, nerve conduction, self-replicating systems)?